CHRISTIAN PERSPECTIVES

Libby Ahluwalia

Foundation Edition

GCSE Religious Studies

OCR
RECOGNISING ACHIEVEMENT

Hodder & Stoughton
A MEMBER OF THE HODDER HEADLINE GROUP

ACKNOWLEDGEMENTS

The author and publishers thank the following for permission to reproduce copyright photographs in this book:
Ian Smeeton pp 2, 4, 5, 97; Bildarchiv Preussischer Kulturbesitz p 8; 'The Baptism of Christ' by Piero della Francesca, © The National Gallery, London p 9; Jenny Matthews/Format p 12; Stephanie Maze/Corbis p 13; Nicola Sutton/Life File p 13; Angela Maynard/Life File p 14; 'The Fall from Grace' by Lucas Cranach the elder, Schlesw.-Holst Landesmuseum, AKG London, p 15; RW Jones/Corbis p 17; Fotografia, Inc/Corbis p 19, Melanie Friend/Format p 20; Mother's Union p 25; Mary Evans Picture Library p 28; 'The creation of Adam' by Michelangelo Buonarroti, Sistine Chapel, AKG London p 30; Penny Tweedie/Corbis p 31; Nicola Sutton/Life File p 32; Aubrey J. Slaughter/Life File p 33; Nicola Sutton/Life File p 35; Ulrike Preuss/Format p 37; Neil Bromhall/Science Photo Library p 39; PA Photos/EPA p 42; The Samaritans p 45; St Christopher's Hospice p 49; Macmillan Cancer Relief p 50; Ulrike Preuss/Format p 53; Amel Emric Stringer/Associated Press p 54; Mary Evans Picture Library p 55; Popperfoto p 56; 57; AP/Andre Camara/STR p 58; Hulton Deutsch p 59top; Associated Press p 59btm; Popperfoto p 60; Associated Press pp iii & 61; Brenda Prince/Format p 65; Jacky Chapman/Format p 66; Brenda Prince/Format p 67; Emma Lee/Life File p 68; Emmanuel Ortiz/Corbis p 72; Bibliotheque Nationale p 75; Imperial War Museum p 76; National Archives p 77; Jeff Widener/Associated Press p 79; Leif Skoogfors/Corbis p 81; Amnesty International pp 82, 83; NASA p 86; Nancy Sefton/Science Photo Library p 88; Jerry Schad/Science Photo Library p 88; 'The Gleaners' by J.F. Millet, Musee d'Orsay, Erich Lessing/AKG London p 89; Mark Edwards/Still Pictures p 90; Tim Davis/Science Photo Library p 91; John Heseltine/Corbis p 92;Barry Mayes/Life File p 94; Associated Press p 98; Pavel Rahman Stringer/Associated Press p 99; Jim Loring/Tearfund p 101; Fairtrade p 102; Robert van der Hilst/Corbis p 103; Christian Aid p 104; CAFOD p 104; The Salvation Army p 105; Stefan Rousseau/PA p 108; Peter Turnley/Corbis p 110; Rajendra Shaw/Traidcraft p 111; Christian Aid p 112; Christian Aid/Nick Davies p 112; Liba Taylor/Action Aid p 113; CAFOD p 114; Jon Spaull/CAFOD p 115; Geoff Crawford/Tearfund p 116; Adam Woolfitt/Corbis p 121; 'Christ on the cross' by Peter Paul Rubens, Copenhagen, Statens Museum for Art, Erich Lessing/ AKG London p 122; copyright © BBC p 123; ©SAF and Christmas Films MCMXCIX all rights reserved. Courtesy of Icon Film Distribution Ltd. p 125.

Every effort has been made to trace and acknowledge ownership of copyright. The publishers will be glad to make suitable arrangements with any copyright holders whom it has not been possible to contact.

Note about the Internet links in the book. The user should be aware that URLs or web addresses change regularly. Every effort has been made to ensure the accuracy of the URLs provided in this book on going to press. It is inevitable, however, that some will change. It is sometimes possible to find a relocated web page, by just typing in the address of the home page for a website in the URL window of your browser.

Orders: please contact Bookpoint Ltd, 130 Milton Park, Abingdon, Oxon OX14 4SB.
Telephone: (44) 01235 827720. Fax: (44) 01235 400454. Lines are open from 9.00 – 6.00, Monday to Saturday, with a 24 hour message answering service. You can also order through our website www.hodderheadline.co.uk.

British Library Cataloguing in Publication Data
A catalogue record for this title is available from the British Library

ISBN 0 340 872 34 9

First Published 2003
Impression number   10 9 8 7 6 5 4 3 2 1
Year   2009 2008 2007 2006 2005 2004 2003

Copyright © Libby Ahluwalia, 2003

All rights reserved. No part of this publication may be reproduced or transmitted in any form or by any means, electronic or mechanical, including photocopy, recording, or any information storage and retrieval system, without permission in writing from the publisher or under licence from the Copyright Licensing Agency Limited. Further details of such licences (for reprographic reproduction) may be obtained from the Copyright Licensing Agency Limited, of 90 Tottenham Court Road, London W1T 4LP.

Cover photo © Stephanie Maze/CORBIS.
Typeset by Dorchester Typesetting, Dorchester, Dorset.
Printed in Italy for Hodder & Stoughton Educational, a division of Hodder Headline Ltd, 338 Euston Road, London NW1 3BH.

CONTENTS

1. Background 2
2. Marriage and Divorce: Relationships within the Family 12
3. Birth and Death 28
4. Prejudice and Equality 52
5. War, Peace and Human Rights 72
6. Christian Responsibility for the Planet 86
7. Christian Responsibility towards Disadvantaged People 96
8. Religion, the Media and Entertainment 118

BACKGROUND

INTRODUCTION

Most people think it is important to do the right thing. Sometimes, everyone agrees about right and wrong. Most people think it is wrong to be cruel to animals, or to drink and drive. But there are a lot of issues where people find it hard to agree about the right thing to do.

How do Christians know what is right and what is wrong? Is there any way of knowing what is the right opinion, or the right thing to do? Or is it just personal opinion?

> **FOR DISCUSSION**
>
> Try to make a list of things that you think are always wrong, in everyone's opinion.

THE IMPORTANCE OF THE BIBLE

Christians believe the Bible is the most important book that was ever written, and they think it teaches a lot about right and wrong. They believe that the Bible comes from God.

In the book of Exodus in the Old Testament, there are many rules and laws. Christians and Jews believe that these were given to Moses by God. The laws are about many different issues, such as the right way to worship God, the right way to treat strangers and the right things to do with money. The most important rules are the **Ten Commandments**:

For most Christians, the Bible is an important source of information about right and wrong

> *Then God spoke all these words:*
>
> *I am the* LORD *your God, who brought you out of the land of Egypt, out of the house of slavery;* **you shall have no other gods** *before me.*
>
> **You shall not make for yourself an idol**, *whether in the form of anything that is in heaven above, or that is on the earth beneath, or that is in the water under the earth. You shall not bow down to them or worship them; for I the* LORD *your God am a jealous God, punishing children for the iniquity*

> *of parents, to the third and the fourth generation of those who reject me, but showing steadfast love to the thousandth generation of those who love me and keep my commandments.*
>
> **You shall not make wrongful use of the name of the LORD your God**, *for the LORD will not acquit anyone who misuses his name.*
>
> **Remember the sabbath day, and keep it holy.** *Six days you shall labour and do all your work. But the seventh day is a sabbath to the LORD your God; you shall not do any work – you, your son or your daughter, your male or female slave, your livestock, or the alien resident in your towns. For in six days the LORD made heaven and earth, the sea, and all that is in them, but rested the seventh day; therefore the LORD blessed the sabbath day and consecrated it.*
>
> **Honour your father and your mother**, *so that your days may be long in the land that the LORD your God is giving you.*
>
> **You shall not murder.**
>
> **You shall not commit adultery.**
>
> **You shall not steal.**
>
> **You shall not bear false witness against your neighbour.**
>
> **You shall not covet** *your neighbour's house; you shall not covet your neighbour's wife, or male or female slave, or ox, or donkey, or anything that belongs to your neighbour.* (Exodus 20: 1–17)

Christians believe that the Ten Commandments are important for everyone, in all parts of the world and at all times in history.

The New Testament also tells Christians how to behave in the right way. The Gospels tell the story of the life, death and rising again of Jesus. They give many examples of Jesus' teaching about right and wrong.

In Matthew's Gospel, chapters 5–7 contain some of the teaching of Jesus about the right way to live. This is called the **Sermon on the Mount**. Here are some examples:

> *You have heard that it was said to the people long ago, 'Do not commit murder, and anyone who murders will be subject to judgement.' But I tell you that anyone who is angry with his brother will be subject to judgement.*
>
> (Matthew 5: 21–22)
>
> *If someone forces you to go one mile, go with him two miles. Give to the one who asks you, and do not turn away from the one who wants to borrow from you.*
>
> (Matthew 5: 41–42)
>
> *No one can serve two masters. Either he will hate the one and love the other, or he will be devoted to the one and despise the other. You cannot serve both God and Money.*
>
> (Matthew 6: 24)

Christians believe that these teachings are very important, because they believe that Jesus was the Son of God. They think that when Jesus spoke, he told people how God wanted them to live. It was not just the opinion of an ordinary human being.

Some Christians try to choose the right thing to do by asking themselves what Jesus would have done. If they think Jesus would not have told a lie, or they think Jesus would have forgiven someone, then they can do the same.

The New Testament contains letters written to some of the very first Christians. They had started churches, and were trying to live together as Christians, but they did not know much about the Christian faith. The letters explain how to live a good life as a Christian, and people still use the teaching in these letters today.

For example, the letter to the church in Ephesus tells people:

CHRISTIAN PERSPECTIVES

> *But among you there must not be even a hint of sexual immorality, or any kind of impurity, or of greed, because they are improper for God's holy people. Nor should there be obscenity, foolish talk or coarse joking, which are out of place, but rather thanksgiving.*
>
> (Ephesians 5: 3–4)

Most Christians believe that reading the Bible is one of the best ways of knowing right from wrong. But they do not always agree about what the Bible means. Some people think that every word of the Bible came straight from God. Other people believe that human writers used their own thinking and ideas, as well as ideas from God, and they might have written things that were for their own times but do not really work today.

Christians always have to think when they are trying to use the teaching of the Bible and apply it to today's world. Sometimes, this can be quite difficult:

- Some problems today were not problems when the Bible was written, so the Bible does not teach about these things. For example, people did not know about global warming, and they did not have nuclear weapons. Christians have to try and work out how the Bible could be used to help with issues like these, but they do not always agree about the right answers.
- Sometimes the Bible says different things about the same topic. For example, some parts of the Bible seem to say that it can be right to fight in a war, but other parts say that people should love their enemies.

Most Christians try to read the Bible often. Some keep a special time of day for reading the Bible quietly on their own. They might also use a book that suggests which part of the Bible to read, and explains it, and gives some questions to think about. Sometimes, Christians want to use the Bible to read about a topic that interests them, so they might look up the passage that they want. Sometimes, groups of Christians meet in each other's homes or at

Sometimes Christians meet together at each other's houses, to study the Bible together and to give each other support

work, and they read the Bible together and talk about what they think it means.

All Christian churches use the Bible in services. Everyone listens and someone reads out a passage from the Bible. Often, the preacher will talk about the Bible passage in the sermon.

Christians use the Bible a lot, but they do not always agree about what it means for today. Different Christian churches sometimes have different opinions. For example, the Roman Catholic Church and the Methodist Church disagree about contraception (birth control). Even in just one church, people will have different opinions about right and wrong.

THE ROLE OF THE CHURCH

Most Christians belong to a church, so that they can share their faith with other Christians. They go to services on Sundays, and sometimes at other times as well. The Church can help people with moral issues:

- People go to church to learn about how to understand the Bible. The church leaders often go to training college, so that they know more about the Bible and can share it with others.
- The minister or priest helps people if they have problems. If someone does not know what to do about a problem, he or she can talk to the minister or priest about it. They might pray about it together, and think about the right way to deal with the problem.
- In the Roman Catholic Church, people who have moral problems can go to confession. If they feel they have done something wrong, they can tell the priest, and the priest will tell them the best way to show they are really sorry.

The Church plays an important part in the lives of Christians. They can learn about moral issues at Sunday services, but they might not all share the same views

CHRISTIAN PERSPECTIVES

Churches often offer all kinds of activities and support groups for their members and for the community

- Many churches run different groups for people with different interests. There might be a men's group or a group for parents and toddlers. These groups can help people when they have to decide between right and wrong, because they give people a chance to talk about things with other Christians.
- Sometimes, Christian Churches decide to make a statement about a moral issue, such as war or abortion. A group of people from the Church get together and discuss the issue first. Christians might use these statements if they have to decide between right and wrong, because they can see what other members of their Church have decided.

PRAYER

Christians believe that prayer is a way of talking to God and listening to God, so it is a very important part of life for them. Sometimes they pray with other people (**communal prayer**) and sometimes they pray quietly on their own (**private prayer**). The Quakers (whose proper name is the Religious Society of Friends) have meetings which are often silent, so that people can think and listen to God.

If Christians have a hard choice to make, one of the first things they will do is pray about it. Most Christians do not hear God speaking to them as a voice, telling them what to do, but they often feel that God shows them the right choices to make in other ways. For example, if a married woman was unhappy and thinking about getting a divorce, she might pray about it. If she saw something in the newspaper saying that divorce can hurt the children, and then saw something on television about marriage counselling, she might believe that this was how God had answered her prayers.

Christians believe that praying to God helps them whenever they have a difficult decision to make

CONSCIENCE

Most people use their consciences when they choose between right and wrong, whether or not they are Christian. The conscience is sometimes described as a 'voice', making people feel guilty when they have done something wrong. Many people feel that they just know what is the right thing to do. Some Christians believe that the conscience comes from God, and is God's way of telling people how to behave.

CHRISTIAN PERSPECTIVES

Some Christians have felt very strong messages from their consciences, and they have chosen to do what they thought was right, even if in put them in danger. For example, Dietrich Bonhoeffer was a Christian who lived at the time of the Second World War. He believed that it was right for him to join a plot to kill Hitler. His conscience told him that it was the right way to put his Christian beliefs into action, fighting evil and looking after people who were weak. Bonhoeffer was found out before he had time to carry out his plans, and he was executed.

Dietrich Bonhoeffer was a Christian whose conscience led him to become involved in a plan to kill Hitler

THE HOLY SPIRIT

Christians believe that there is only one God. They believe God can be understood in three different ways – this is called the **doctrine of the Trinity**. Christians believe that God can be understood as the **Father** and maker of the world. He can also be understood as the **Son**, who came to earth as Jesus. He can also be understood as the **Holy Spirit**. The Holy Spirit is the part of God that lives in every Christian. It helps them when they are afraid, or when they are unhappy, or when they have choices to make. Christians believe that if they ask the Holy Spirit to help them with their problems, they are more likely to choose the right answer.

The Holy Spirit is difficult to describe. Often, in pictures it is shown as a dove. In the Bible, when Jesus was baptized, the Holy Spirit was said to come down like a dove:

BACKGROUND

> At that time Jesus came from Nazareth in Galilee and was baptised by John in the Jordan. As Jesus was coming up out of the water, he saw heaven and earth being torn open and the Spirit descending on him like a dove.
>
> (Mark 1: 9–10)

The dove is also a sign of peace. In the story of Noah, there was a great flood over all the earth. When Noah wanted to find out if the flood was over, he sent out a dove to look for dry land. The dove came back with an olive branch in its mouth. Christians use the sign of a dove to show the belief that God will make everything all right.

AGAPE

Christians believe God is love. They believe they should show this by being loving to each other.

When Jesus was asked which of the Old Testament laws he thought was the greatest, he chose two:

In Christian art, the Holy Spirit is often shown as a dove. Baptism of Christ, *by Piero della Francesca*

> One of the teachers of the law came and heard them debating. Noticing that Jesus had given them a good answer, he asked him, 'Of all the commandments, which is the most important?'
>
> 'The most important one,' answered Jesus, 'is this: "Hear, O Israel, the Lord our God, the Lord is one. **Love the Lord your God** with all your heart and with all your soul and with all your mind and with all your strength." The second is this: "**Love your neighbour as yourself.**" There is no commandment greater than these.'
>
> 'Well said, teacher,' the man replied. 'You are right in saying that God is one and there is no other but him. To love him with all your heart, with all your understanding and with all your strength, and to love your neighbour as yourself is more important than all burnt offerings and sacrifices.'
>
> When Jesus saw that he had answered wisely, he said to him, 'You are not far from the kingdom of God.' And from then on no one dared ask him any more questions.
>
> (Mark 12: 28–34)

CHRISTIAN PERSPECTIVES

There are two parts to this teaching. Christians should love God, and they should love their neighbours.

Loving God means putting God first, and trying to do what God wants. It means spending time with God and talking and listening to God. Loving your neighbour means treating other people as equals, the way you would like to be treated yourself. This is called the Golden Rule:

> *So in everything, **do to others what you would have them do to you**, for this sums up the Law and the Prophets.* (Matthew 7: 12)

The Christian idea of love is called **agape**. This is a Greek word. The Greeks had different words for different kinds of love:

- **Eros** is the name for sexual love.
- **Philos** is the name for love of a brother or close friend.
- **Storge** is the name for family love and loyalty.

So somebody might feel **eros** for a boyfriend or girlfriend, or even for someone from the television. They might feel **philos** for their best friend, and they might feel **storge** for their cousins, even if they do not see them very often. Sometimes, people feel more than one kind of love for the same person. In marriages that work really well, the husband and wife might feel all kinds of love for each other.

Christians believe that all love comes from God. They believe the most important kind of love is one called **agape**.

Agape is love for other people, no matter what they are like. It means loving people whatever they look like, and however they behave. It means caring about other people and wanting the best for them.

Agape love is very important in all Christian teaching. Christians believe that God does not just think love is a good thing – they believe that God *is* love.

> *Dear friends, let us love one another, for love comes from God. Everyone who loves has been born of God and knows God. Whoever does not love does not know God, because **God is love**.*
>
> *This is how God showed his love among us: He sent his one and only Son into the world that we might live through him.*
>
> *This is love: not that we loved God, but that **he loved us and sent his Son** as an atoning sacrifice for our sins.*
>
> *Dear friends, since God so loved us, we also ought to love one another.*
>
> *No-one has ever seen God; but if we love one another, God lives in us and his love is made complete in us . . . We love because he first loved us.*
>
> *If anyone says, 'I love God,' yet hates his brother, he is a liar. For anyone who does not love his brother, whom he has seen, cannot love God, whom he has not seen.*
>
> *And he has given us this command: **Whoever loves God must also love his brother**.*
> (1 John 4: 7–21)

This passage comes from a letter sent to one of the very first churches in the early days of Christianity. John says that people should try to live together with love. If they do this, they will be sharing God with each other. John also said that the love of God is proved, because God sent Jesus into the world and took away the guilt of human sin.

Paul wrote about love in his letter to the church in Corinth. The people in that church had many arguments with each other. Paul tried to tell them about agape love. Many Christians choose this passage to be read in church when they get married, because it is so beautiful:

BACKGROUND

If I speak in the tongues of men and of angels, but have not love, I am only a resounding gong or a clanging cymbal.

If I have the gift of prophecy and can fathom all mysteries and all knowledge, and if I have a faith that can move mountains, but have not love, I am nothing.

If I give all I possess to the poor and surrender my body to the flames, but have not love, I gain nothing.

Love is patient, love is kind*. It does not envy, it does not boast, it is not proud.*

It is not rude, it is not self-seeking, it is not easily angered, it keeps no record of wrongs.

Love does not delight in evil *but rejoices with the truth.*

It always protects, always trusts, always hopes, always perseveres.

Love never fails*. But where there are prophecies, they will cease; where there are tongues, they will be stilled; where there is knowledge, it will pass away.*

For we know in part and we prophesy in part, but when perfection comes, the imperfect disappears.

When I was a child, I talked like a child, I thought like a child, I reasoned like a child. When I became a man, I put childish ways behind me.

Now we see but a poor reflection as in a mirror; then we shall see face to face. Now I know in part; then I shall know fully, even as I am fully known.

And now these three remain: faith, hope and love. ***But the greatest of these is love****.*

(1 Corinthians 13)

St Augustine was one of the great thinkers in Christian history. He lived in the fifth century CE. He did not want people to think that being a Christian was all about following rules. He thought that doing the right thing was much easier than that. Augustine said 'Love, and then do what you will'. He meant that you can do what you want, as long as you act in a loving way.

In the 1960s, a Christian called Joseph Fletcher wrote a book called *Situation Ethics*, using the same idea. He said that if you try to do the most loving thing, then you will make the right choices. But not everyone agreed with him. Some people said that Christians might not always know what is the most loving thing to do, and they could get it wrong. They said Christians need the Bible and Church teaching as well.

SUMMARY

Most Christians use several different ways of telling right from wrong:

- They use the teaching of the Bible.
- They use the advice of the Church and their Christian friends.
- They use their consciences and pray that the Holy Spirit will help them.
- They try to do what Jesus would have done.
- They try to show agape love for other people.

MARRIAGE AND DIVORCE: RELATIONSHIPS WITHIN THE FAMILY

The importance of family life for Christians, and Christian views about the roles of family members. Christian teaching about divorce and annulment, and different Christian opinions about marriage after divorce.

There are many different kinds of families. Some have two parents and their children. Some have one parent, or stepparents, or foster children, or no children. Some old people live with their adult sons and daughters. Christians know that families are all different.

Families are all different. This family has adopted children, and two parents

Some religions teach that all adults should marry and have children. But Christianity teaches that some people can choose to stay single. Some of the most famous Christians have not married. Christians might choose to give their lives to God in other ways, such as being a priest, or a monk, or a nun. Jesus never married. Some single Christians do important work that does not fit in with family life, such as being a doctor or nurse in a country where there is a war and they are in danger.

MARRIAGE AND DIVORCE: RELATIONSHIPS WITHIN THE FAMILY

- The family is the first place where children can find out about love and getting on with other people. They learn this through living with their parents and their brothers and sisters.
- Families can help the community. They can give other people a place to stay. They can support other families. They can look after old people or adopt children who need parents.

Some Christians never marry, but give their lives to God in other ways

Christians believe that family life is important, because families give each other love and support. Families are important in religion:

- They are a place where children can learn. Families train children to become good adults. Christian families can go to church together, and they can encourage each other to stay in the Christian faith. Parents can set a good example to their children and show them how to live a Christian life; for example, they can invite lonely people to their home, or help the children raise money for charity. They can teach the children about Christian festivals.

Families are where we learn about love and getting on with each other

- Christians believe that the family is a very important part of society. Most think that newspapers and television should not give people the idea that all families are unhappy or all marriages go wrong (see Chapter 8).

CHRISTIAN PERSPECTIVES

LIVING TOGETHER

FOR DISCUSSION

Do you think that Christianity should change its views about couples who live together without being married, to keep more up to date?

The number of weddings of people getting married for the first time has been falling since the 1970s. Today, many couples choose to live together without getting married. They might plan to marry one day, or they might not see the point in getting married. Some people think it is wrong to promise to love someone for ever, because you do not know how you will feel in ten or twenty years' time. They might say that living together helps them to treat their partners well, because if they treat them badly, then there is no reason for them to stay. Divorce costs a lot of money, but splitting up if you have been living together is much cheaper. It is quite common today for people to have children without being married.

But many Christians believe that marriage is still important. They might say that a couple can only really trust each other when they are married. Christians might say that people who are married will remember the promises they have made to each other and will try harder to sort out problems. They might also say that it is best for children to be brought up by two parents who are married to each other, and that this is what God wants.

Many Christians also say that sex should only happen between two people who are married to each other. Roman Catholics believe that God made sex to join a married couple together and to give them children. Sex outside marriage, such as sex between couples who are living together, might be seen as wrong, because the real purpose of sex is to show married love. But many people think that there is a difference between having sex with someone you love, and having sex with someone you do not know very well, for example after meeting at a party or on holiday.

Christians believe that there is still an important place for marriage in modern society

MARRIAGE AND DIVORCE: RELATIONSHIPS WITHIN THE FAMILY

BIBLICAL TEACHING ABOUT MARRIAGE

The Bible teaches that marriage is something very special. In the story of the Creation, God makes Eve as a partner for Adam:

> So the LORD God caused the man to fall into a deep sleep; and while he was sleeping, he took one of the man's ribs and closed up the place with flesh. Then **the LORD God made a woman from the rib he had taken out of the man**, and he brought her to the man.
> The man said, 'This is now bone of my bones and flesh of my flesh; she shall be called "woman", for she was taken out of a man.'
> For this reason a man will leave his father and mother and be united to his wife, and they will become one flesh.
> (Genesis 2: 21–24)

The writers of the Bible show their belief that God always wanted men and women to be joined together as couples. When they have children, God's creation continues.

The Bible teaches that marriage should be taken very seriously. It says that husbands and wives should be faithful to each other. One of the Ten Commandments is:

> You shall not commit adultery. (Exodus 20: 14)

Christians believe that husbands and wives should be faithful to each other because adultery breaks the promises they make to each other when they marry.

In a story in John's Gospel, a woman is caught committing adultery, and is about to be killed for breaking the law. Jesus surprises the crowd with his attitude to this:

The book of Genesis teaches that God always intended men and women to be partners for each other. The fall from Space by Lucas Cranach

CHRISTIAN PERSPECTIVES

> *The teachers of the law and the Pharisees brought in a woman caught in adultery. They made her stand before the group and said to Jesus, 'Teacher, this woman was caught in the act of adultery. In the Law Moses commanded us to stone such women. Now what do you say?'*
>
> *They were using this question as a trap, in order to have a basis for accusing him. But Jesus bent down and started to write on the ground with his finger.*
>
> *When they kept on questioning him, he straightened up and said to them, **'If any one of you is without sin, let him be the first to throw a stone at her.'***
>
> *Again he stooped down and wrote on the ground.*
>
> *At this, those who heard began to go away one at a time, the older ones first, until only Jesus was left, with the woman still standing there.*
>
> *Jesus straightened up and asked her, 'Woman, where are they? Has no one condemned you?'*
>
> *'No one, sir,' she said. 'Then neither do I condemn you,' Jesus declared. 'Go now and leave your life of sin.'*
>
> (John 8: 3–11)

FOR DISCUSSION

Do you think people can stay faithful to each other all their lives? Is there anything wrong with adultery, if the other partner never finds out about it?

Jesus taught that adultery is a serious sin, but people should show forgiveness to each other.

A CHRISTIAN MARRIAGE

If two people want to get married in a Christian church, the priest or minister will talk to them about what marriage means. They will talk about the promises they are going to make, so that they understand them. The Church of England teaches that marriage is a gift from God:

> *Marriage is given, that husband and wife may comfort and help each other, living faithfully together in need and in plenty, in sorrow and in joy. It is given, that with delight and tenderness they may know each other in love, and, through the joy of their bodily union, may strengthen the union of their hearts and lives. It is given as the foundation of family life in which children may be born and nurtured in accordance with God's will, to his praise and glory.*
>
> (Common Worship 2000)

MARRIAGE AND DIVORCE: RELATIONSHIPS WITHIN THE FAMILY

In the Roman Catholic Church, marriage is one of the **sacraments**. This means it is one of the ways that people can see a sign of God's love for people. In marriage, the love between a husband and wife shows something of the love of God.

Christians believe that marriage is important because in a marriage, people learn about love. They learn about forgiving, looking after each other, and caring about each other's feelings. They believe that in marriage, they learn more about God, because God is love (1 John 4).

Through a loving marriage, Christians believe they learn something about the love of God

CHRISTIAN PERSPECTIVES

DIFFERENT ROLES WITHIN THE FAMILY

The Bible teaches that there are right ways of behaving for different members of a family.

THE ROLES OF HUSBANDS AND WIVES

Some Christians think that a wife should do what her husband tells her. She should support him and look after their children. They think the man should be in charge. He should look after his wife and children, and earn the money. They believe this is what the Bible teaches. They also think that it is important for one person to be the leader, so that they can settle arguments. Men have stronger bodies than women, and women give birth to babies, so some people say it is natural for the man to be the leader and for the woman to have a caring role.

In the New Testament, Paul explains his views about husbands and wives:

Some Christians believe that the role of the husband should be to provide for his family, and the role of the wife should be to support him and look after the children

> **For the husband is the head of the wife** as Christ is the head of the church, his body, of which he is the Saviour.
> Now as the church submits to Christ, so also **wives should submit to their husbands** in everything.
> **Husbands, love your wives**, just as Christ loved the church and gave himself up for her to make her holy, cleansing her by the washing with water through the word, and to present her to himself as a radiant church, without stain or wrinkle or any other blemish, but holy and blameless.
> In this same way, **husbands ought to love their wives** as their own bodies. He who loves his wife loves himself.
> (Ephesians 5: 22–24)

Here, Paul says that he thinks the man should be the leader in a marriage. He says a husband and wife should be like Christ and the Church, and the man should be in charge. This does not mean that he can bully his wife, or make her do all the work. He has to respect her and love her. But Paul thinks that the wife should do as her husband says. In some Christian marriage services, the bride promises to obey her new husband, following

MARRIAGE AND DIVORCE: RELATIONSHIPS WITHIN THE FAMILY

this teaching from the Bible.

Other Christians believe these views are too old-fashioned. The Bible was written long ago, when society was different. Most women today do not promise to obey their husbands when they get married in church. Many people think that men and women should be equal at home and at work. They think they should both look after the children, and should both be able to go out to work. It does not have to be the man who is always in charge.

Christians might support this view with teaching from the Bible. They might use the passage in Genesis which says everyone is made 'in the image of God', to show that all people are equal. They might use this verse from the letter to the Galatians:

> *There is neither Jew nor Greek, slave nor free, **male nor female**, for you **are all** one in Christ Jesus.*
>
> (Galatians 3: 28)

In this passage, Paul says that Christians should not think too much about how people are different. They should see that their faith brings them together as equals. In the home, this could mean that they share the work and both have an equal say.

Many Christians believe that parents should share childcare and housework, and that mothers as well as fathers should be able to go out to work

CHRISTIAN PERSPECTIVES

LOOK UP
1 Peter 3: 1– 2, and verse 7

IN YOUR NOTES
(a) What does this passage say about why wives should do what their husbands say?
(b) How are husbands told to treat their wives?
(c) Some Christians think that wives should obey their husbands. What reasons might they give? Other Christians disagree. What reasons might they give?

FOR DISCUSSION
What do you think Christians should do, if they have a relative who is too old and ill to live on their own? Should they let them live in a nursing home? Or do they have a duty to bring them into their own homes to live, even if that is very difficult?

Caring for relatives is an important responsibility for Christians

THE ROLES OF CHILDREN AND PARENTS
The Bible teaches that Christians should respect their parents. They should think about what their parents want:

> *Honour your father and your mother, so that you may live long in the land the LORD your God is giving you.* (Exodus 20: 12)

Adults should look after elderly members of the family, and make sure they have everything they need:

> *If anyone does not provide for his relatives, and especially for his immediate family, he has denied the faith and is worse than an unbeliever.* (1 Timothy 5: 8)

Parents, too, are responsible for their children. They should teach them about their faith and bring them up to behave well:

> *Discipline your son, and he will give you peace; he will bring delight to your soul.* (Proverbs 29: 17)

But they should not be too hard on them:

MARRIAGE AND DIVORCE: RELATIONSHIPS WITHIN THE FAMILY

> *Children, obey your parents in everything, for this pleases the Lord.*
> *Fathers, do not embitter your children, or they will become discouraged.* (Colossians 3: 20–21)

The Bible teaches that family members should show special care for each other. There are stories in the Bible that show what can happen if family members treat each other badly.

In the story of Cain and Abel (Genesis 4), and in the story of Joseph and his brothers (Genesis 37), jealousy between brothers goes too far and they want to kill each other. In the story of David and Bathsheba (2 Samuel 11–12), David commits adultery, and everything goes wrong. These and other stories show that families do have problems, and they show what can happen if people let their feelings get out of control.

There are also stories in the Bible that show the good side of family life. The book of Ruth tells a story of love and loyalty. In the book of Proverbs, there is a beautiful passage about a good wife:

> *A wife of noble character who can find?* **She is worth far more than rubies.**
> *Her husband has full confidence in her and lacks nothing of value.*
> *She brings him good, not harm, all the days of her life.*
> *She selects wool and flax and works with eager hands.*
> *She is like the merchant ships, bringing her food from afar.*
> *She gets up while it is still dark; she provides food for her family and portions for her servant girls.*
> *She considers a field and buys it; out of her earnings she plants a vineyard.*
> *She sets about her work vigorously; her arms are strong for her tasks.*
> *She sees that her trading is profitable, and her lamp does not go out at night.*
> *In her hand she holds the distaff and grasps the spindle with her fingers.*
> *She opens her arms to the poor and extends her hands to the needy.*
> *When it snows, she has no fear for her household; for all of them are clothed in scarlet.*
> *She makes coverings for her bed; she is clothed in fine linen and purple.*
> *Her husband is respected at the city gate, where he takes his seat among the elders of the land.*
> *She makes linen garments and sells them, and supplies the merchants with sashes.*
> *She is clothed with strength and dignity; she can laugh at the days to come.*
> *She speaks with wisdom, and faithful instruction is on her tongue.*
> *She watches over the affairs of her household and does not eat the bread of idleness.*
> *Her children arise and call her blessed; her husband also, and he praises her:*
> *'Many women do noble things, but you surpass them all.'* (Proverbs 31: 10–29)

The Bible says that people should try to treat everyone, even strangers, as if they were family. They should not just care about their own families. They should remember that everyone is made by God, and they should show Christian love (agape) to everyone they meet:

> *Whoever does God's will is my brother and sister and mother.* (Mark 3: 35)
> *Do not rebuke an older man harshly, but exhort him as if he were your father. Treat younger men as brothers, older women as mothers, and younger women as sisters, with absolute purity.*
> (1 Timothy 5: 1–2)

CHRISTIAN PERSPECTIVES

DIVORCE

Christians think that marriage is very important. But not all marriages are happy. There are very few marriages where both partners agree, all the time, about everything. Arguments are a normal part of married life. In a marriage that works, the couple learn to get on together even if they disagree about some things.

Arguments are normal in married life, but sometimes a couple decide they do not want to stay married

But sometimes, a husband and wife know they are making each other too unhappy, so they decide to separate. Marriages can break down for many reasons:

- One or both of the partners might meet someone else, and have an affair. They might not be able to trust each other again, or they might decide to go and live with the new person.
- Money can be the cause of trouble in a marriage. Sometimes, one partner likes to save carefully and the other likes to spend a lot. This can cause arguments.
- Sometimes, people expect their marriage to be perfect, and find it hard to cope if there are any problems.
- Children often bring married people closer together. But sometimes they can be the cause of problems too, if the couple have different ideas about how to bring up children.
- Sometimes, people just change as they grow older, and they might not have as much in common as they once did.

It is always difficult when a marriage does not work. It is even harder when there are children. Often, the children have to try not to take sides, and they have to get used to having two different homes.

DIVORCE AND THE LAW

If a couple do not want to stay married any more, they might apply for a divorce. In the past, divorce was more difficult. Today, people can be divorced more easily. They no longer have to prove that one partner is to blame for the things that went wrong. Some people think this helps people to get divorced more peacefully, but other people think divorce has been made too easy.

FOR DISCUSSION

Do you think that people would try harder to make their marriages work if divorce became more difficult?

BIBLICAL TEACHING ABOUT DIVORCE

Divorce is allowed in the teaching of the Old Testament in the Bible. If a man wanted to divorce his wife, he had to put it in writing:

> *If a man marries a woman who becomes displeasing to him because he finds something indecent about her, and* **he writes her a certificate of divorce**, *gives it to her and sends her from his house …*
> (Deuteronomy 24: 1)

But the teaching Jesus gave in the New Testament is different. Mark's Gospel says that the Pharisees asked Jesus a question about divorce:

> *Some Pharisees came and tested him by asking, 'Is it lawful for a man to divorce his wife?'*
> *'What did Moses command you?' he replied.*
> *They said, 'Moses permitted a man to write a certificate of divorce and send her away.'*
> *'It was because your hearts were hard that Moses wrote you this law,' Jesus replied.*
> *'But at the beginning of creation God "made them male and female.*
> *For this reason a man will leave his father and mother and be united to his wife, and the two will become one flesh." So they are no longer two, but one.*
> *Therefore* **what God has joined together, let man not separate.**'
> *When they were in the house again, the disciples asked Jesus about this.*
> *He answered, 'Anyone who divorces his wife and marries another woman commits adultery against her. And if she divorces her husband and marries another man, she commits adultery.'*
> (Mark 10: 2–12)

Jesus gives a very clear teaching here. Marriage is for life, and divorce is not allowed. The Old Testament law is made stricter.

But in Matthew's Gospel, the teaching of Jesus is different:

> *It has been said, 'Anyone who divorces his wife must give her a certificate of divorce.'*
> *But I tell you that anyone who divorces his wife,* **except for marital unfaithfulness**, *causes her to become an adulteress, and anyone who marries the divorced woman commits adultery.*
> (Matthew 5: 31–32)

Here, Jesus says that divorce is wrong unless someone has committed adultery. So divorce could be right in some cases.

It is difficult to know why the Bible has different teachings of Jesus about divorce. Perhaps Jesus said different things about it. Perhaps someone changed what he said, to fit in better with most people's opinion. Perhaps someone made a mistake remembering what Jesus had said.

Because the Bible has these different teachings, the Christian Churches have different views about divorce. Some teach that divorce can never be right. Others teach that in some cases divorce might be the best choice.

CHRISTIAN PERSPECTIVES

CHURCH TEACHING ABOUT REMARRIAGE AFTER DIVORCE

The **Roman Catholic Church** teaches that marriage is a sacrament. It holds people together for life. People who have been married in a Catholic church stay married until one of them dies. They can live apart if they want to, but they are not allowed to divorce.

Some Catholic marriages are annulled. This is different from divorce. When a marriage is annulled, it means that people agree it was not a proper marriage from the start. This can be for several reasons:

- The couple could have been married without understanding what they were doing. For example, the church service might have been in a language one of them did not understand very well.
- They might have been forced into getting married.
- One of the partners might not have wanted children when they got married.
- They might not have had sex as a married couple.

If Roman Catholics want to marry for a second time, when their first husband or wife is still alive, the Catholic Church will not agree to it. The Catholic Church will think it is the same as adultery.

Other Christian Churches, such as the **Church of England** and the **Methodist Church**, do allow divorce. If divorced people want to get married again to new partners, the Churches usually allow this. If they want to get married again in church, the vicar or minister usually agrees, but he or she can say no if it seems that the couple is not taking Christian marriage very seriously.

CHRISTIAN MARRIAGE IN PRACTICE

Christians believe that marriage is part of God's plan for men and women. They might put this Christian belief into practice by trying hard to make their marriages work. They might try to help other couples and families too. They could put their beliefs into practice in different ways:

- They might pray together.
- They will try to use the teaching of the Bible in their family life. Husbands and wives will try to be faithful to each other, and treat each other with respect, and keep the promises they made on their wedding day. They will try to bring up their children to be Christians.
- They might vote for MPs who support family values.
- They might join a group at church that gives support to families. Some churches have special groups for married couples, to help them discuss Christian marriage. The Mothers' Union is a group in the Church of England that works to support family life.

Members of the Mothers' Union do not have to be mothers. They can be married or single, men or women. The aims of the Mothers' Union are:

- to help people understand what Jesus said about family life.
- to help parents bring up their children as Christians.
- to pray for families.
- to help protect children.
- to help families in need.
- to meet with other groups and work together for family life.

MARRIAGE AND DIVORCE: RELATIONSHIPS WITHIN THE FAMILY

If a Christian belongs to the Mothers' Union, he or she might put these beliefs in practice. He or she could: look after babies and small children while their parents go to church; help the families of people in prison; help the local Women's Refuge; babysit for single parents.

Christians might put their beliefs about marriage into practice in other ways. They might support a group, such as Relate or CMAC.

Relate is a group set up to help people who are in relationships. It began during the Second World War. Many people had problems with their marriages in the war. They were apart for a long time, and sometimes things happened to them which made them change. They often found it hard to live together again happily. At first, Relate was called the Marriage Guidance Council. It changed its name because now it is for all sorts of people, whether they are married or not.

Relate gives people a chance to talk about their problems with a trained listener. These listeners are volunteers. Sometimes, both people in the relationship will go to talk as a couple, and they are helped to tell each other about their feelings and talk about what is going wrong. Sometimes, just one person goes. The listener does not give advice, but helps the people to think about what they want to do.

Mothers' Union logo

ICT FOR RESEARCH

Visit the web-site of the Mothers' Union:
http://www.themothersunion.org

IN YOUR NOTES

Describe some of the work of the Mothers' Union.

The Mothers' Union supports family life in many different ways, for example by offering childcare

CHRISTIAN PERSPECTIVES

Some Christians support groups, such as Relate. This gives help to people who are having problems in their relationships

Relate does not always help couples to keep their marriage together. Sometimes, people go there when they have already decided to divorce. They go to talk about the best ways of making sure that the divorce does not cause too much hurt.

People have to pay to use Relate, because the offices and the telephones and advertising all cost money.

Relate is not a Christian organisation. It helps people from all kinds of religions, and from no religion at all. But Christians might choose to support it, because they might think it is a good way of helping people with their marriages.

CMAC is the Catholic Marriage Advisory Council. It tries to help anyone who needs it. They do not have to be Catholic, or married. But most of the volunteers are Catholic. It offers help for people who are planning to get married. It gives advice about natural methods of contraception (see page 33) as well as giving help to people who have problems with their relationships.

Roman Catholics might choose to support CMAC because it is based on Catholic ideas. Its volunteers understand Catholic teaching about marriage, sex, contraception and divorce.

MARRIAGE AND DIVORCE: RELATIONSHIPS WITHIN THE FAMILY

PRACTICE GCSE QUESTIONS

1 (a) **Describe Christian teaching about the way children should treat their parents. (8 marks)**
If a question asks you for Christian teaching, it means you can use teaching from the Bible, or from the church, or from any Christians. Think of some teaching from the Bible that you could use in your answer (look at page 20). Explain what these teachings mean.

(b) **How might a married couple's Christian faith affect the way in which they behave towards each other? (7 marks)**
Remember to think about the question carefully. Explain what Christians believe about marriage, and why it is important. Then try to give some examples of how they might work at keeping the marriage strong (look at page 24).

(c) **'The head of a Christian family should be the father.' Do you agree? Give reasons to support your answer, and show that you have thought about different points of view. (5 marks)**
Notice that you are being asked to write about a Christian family. You need to refer to Christian beliefs, and say what you think a Christian might think. You also need to give a different point of view, and your own view. Try to give reasons for these opinions.

2 (a) **Describe two different Christian beliefs about remarriage after divorce. (8 marks)**
Here, you need to think about two different Christian points of view. It would be sensible to write about the Roman Catholic view, and the view of another Church, such as the Church of England. Try to explain why Catholics believe people should not get married for a second time if their first partner is still alive. Then try to explain why other Churches think it can be allowed.

(b) **Explain how and why a Christian might support the work of an organisation that provides help for people who are having difficulties in their relationships. (7 marks)**
Notice that here you are asked to explain how and why, so you need to do both. For 'how', you should write about how a Christian might support this sort of organisation – for example, they might train to be a listener, or they might raise funds. Then you need to explain 'why', so you could write about why Christians believe marriage and the family are important.

(c) **'There is nothing wrong with living together and having children together without getting married.' Do you agree? Give reasons to support your answer and show that you have thought about different points of view. You must refer to Christianity in your answer. (5 marks)**
You need to include more than one point of view here. Start by saying what a Christian would think about this, because you need to include a Christian point of view. Then give a different point of view – perhaps what someone who was not a Christian would say. Remember to give your own opinion and to support it with reasons.

BIRTH AND DEATH

> Issues related to the sanctity of life, and Christian responses to these issues.
> Issues related to birth control (contraception), fertility treatment (the right to a child and the use of embryos), abortion, suicide, and euthanasia.
> Biblical teachings about the value of human life, and the teachings of the Christian churches.

INTRODUCTION

In the past, medicine did not give people many choices between right and wrong, because there were many things that doctors could do nothing about. Some couples could not have children and so never became parents. Often, more than ten babies were born in the same family. Some lived, and some died. When people came to the ends of their lives, some died in peace and some died in pain. There was not much anyone could do about it.

In the Bible, there are big families like Jacob's, with 12 sons. There are people like Hannah, who could not have a baby. There were people who had been ill for years. Only God could do anything about it.

But since the Bible was written, things have changed. People

In the past, people did not have much choice over life and death. Some people had very big families, whether they liked it or not

BIRTH AND DEATH

can now choose how many children to have. If they cannot have children on their own, doctors can give them fertility treatment. Women who do not want to be pregnant can have safe abortions. Many illnesses can be cured or slowed down. People can be kept alive on life support machines.

These changes have left people with choices to make. Should people be able to make their own choices about life and death, or should it be left to God?

'PLAYING GOD'

Some people say that it is wrong for doctors to make choices about life and death. They think things should be left alone, so that nature can take its course. They say that if doctors interfere, they are 'playing God', and making choices that only God should be able to make.

But this way of thinking does not always help. If we always let nature take its course, we would not be able to use medicine at all. People would be left to die, even though doctors could have helped them.

If someone has diabetes, doctors can give them daily injections of insulin, and this will save their lives. Most people would not want the doctors to do nothing, and let them die. If someone is badly hurt in a road accident, and they will never get better and are on life support, some people say it is wrong for doctors to end the life – they should keep the person alive and not let nature take its course.

People often think that in some cases, the doctors should interfere, but in other cases, they should leave things alone. It is difficult to know when to do something, and when to leave it.

Doctors often have to make difficult choices. It is part of their job. If a baby is born early and has serious problems, doctors have to decide how hard to try to keep that baby alive, when they know it will always be disabled if it lives. If a very old person has a heart attack, doctors have to decide whether to let them die naturally or whether to give them treatment. Sometimes, they have to make these choices quickly and under pressure.

Christians believe it is important to use medical knowledge, and not just do nothing when someone is ill and could be helped. In the Gospels, there are many stories that show Jesus was a healer. The Gospel writer Luke is thought to have been a doctor.

> *While Jesus was in one of the towns, a man came along who was covered with leprosy. When he saw Jesus, he fell with his face to the ground and begged him, 'Lord, if you are willing, you can make me clean.'*
> *Jesus reached out his hand and touched the man. 'I am willing,' he said. 'Be clean!' And immediately the leprosy left him.*
> (Luke 5: 12–13)

Christians see medicine as something good. They believe healing comes from God. But they can also see that medicine raises questions about right and wrong, and they do not always agree about the answers to those questions.

FOR DISCUSSION

Do you think that there are times when a doctor should not interfere with decisions about life and death?

CHRISTIAN PERSPECTIVES

This painting shows the creation of Adam, made 'in the image of God' – Sistine Chapel, Michelangelo

THE SANCTITY OF LIFE

Christians often say that they believe in the **'sanctity of life'**. When they say this, they mean that they believe there is something special and holy about life. Christians believe human life is different from other kinds of life. They believe that people share something of God.

In the book of Genesis, when God made the first man Adam, he 'breathed into his nostrils the breath of life' (Genesis 2: 7). This did not happen with the animals and plants, only with humans.

Genesis also says that people are made 'in the image of God':

> *So God created man **in his own image**, in the image of God he created him; male and female he created them.*
>
> (Genesis 1: 26–27)

Christians believe that human life shows something of God himself. They believe that people have a 'soul', which does not die when the body dies. The soul lives on after death. Christians say that because people have souls, they are different from other animals and their lives are more special.

Some parts of the Bible teach that God knows every person, and plans each life. For example, there is a passage in the book of Psalms which compares God with someone who makes a piece of cloth. It shows the belief

BIRTH AND DEATH

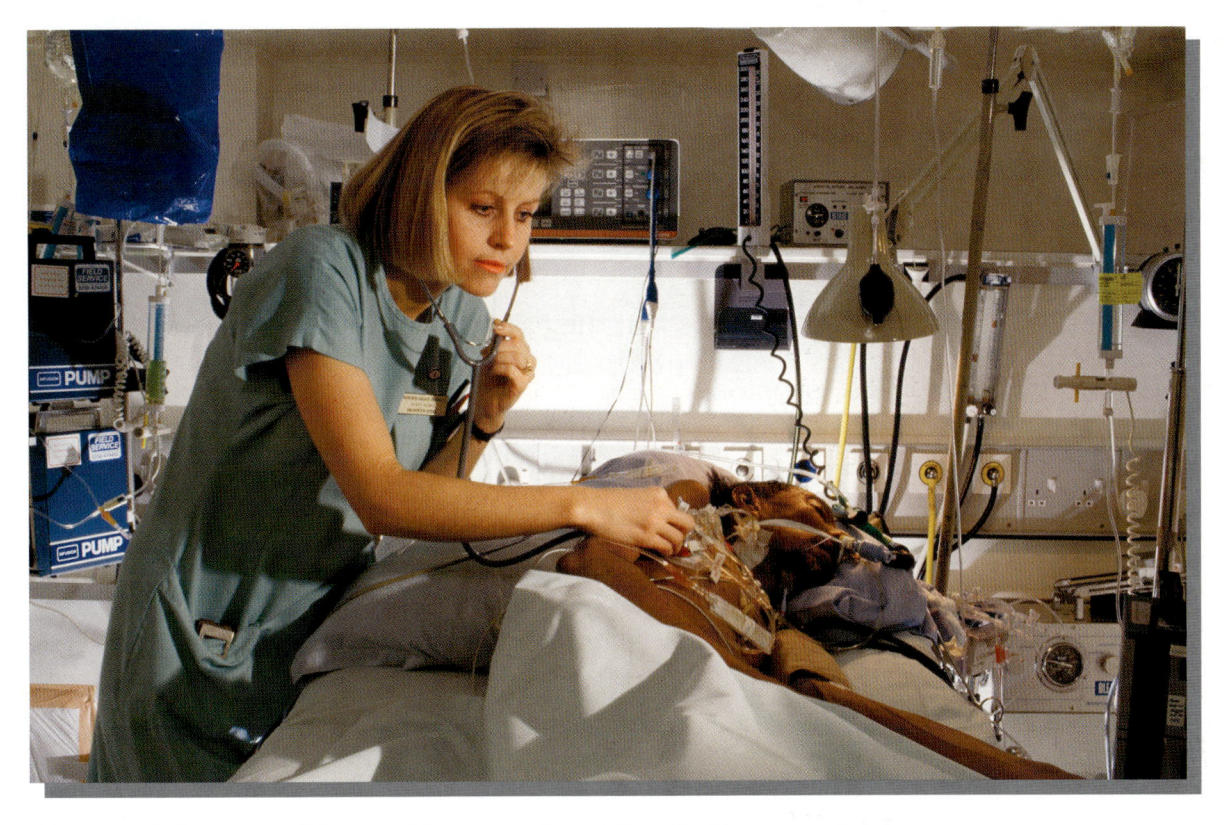

Christians believe that all human life is special, and that God knows each person

that God knows each person as well as a weaver knows the cloth he makes:

> *For you created my inmost being;* **you knit me together in my mother's womb.**
>
> *I praise you because I am fearfully and wonderfully made; your works are wonderful, I know that full well.*
>
> *My frame was not hidden from you when I was made in the secret place. When I was woven together in the depths of the earth,*
>
> *your eyes saw my unformed body. All the days ordained for me were written in your book before one of them came to be.*
>
> (Psalm 139: 13–16)

SUMMARY
- Christians believe that human life is 'sacred'. It is different from other kinds of life.
- Other animals do not have souls. Only humans are made in the image of God.
- Christians believe that God plans each human life.

VALUING HUMAN LIFE
The belief that human life is sacred affects Christians in many ways:

- Christians believe God makes each person to be special, so everyone is important. It does not matter if they are very young or very old, healthy or ill, working people or in need of a lot of care. This means that Christians try to treat all people with respect. Some Christians put their beliefs about the value of human life into practice by becoming doctors or nurses.
- Christians believe that God has given their lives to them. This means they have a duty to take care of themselves. They should try to do some good with their lives and not just waste them. They should take care of their health.

31

CHRISTIAN PERSPECTIVES

In a New Testament letter, Paul writes:

> *Don't you know that you yourselves are God's temple and that God's Spirit lives in you?*
> (1 Corinthians 3: 16)

In the past, Christians thought that suicide was a terrible sin. This was because it seemed to be throwing away God's gift of life. Today, people understand a lot more about the problems that sometimes lead to suicide.

Because Christians believe that life is sacred, it affects their attitude to all sorts of medical issues, such as contraception, abortion and euthanasia. Not all Christians agree about the right answers to these issues.

CONTRACEPTION (Birth Control)

Contraception is sometimes called birth control. Christians do not always agree about it.

In the past, people could not choose how many children to have. Some couples had ten or more. Today, people can choose how many children to have, by using contraception.

THE TEACHING OF THE ROMAN CATHOLIC CHURCH

Roman Catholics believe that artificial contraception is wrong. Artificial contraception is the name for types of contraception which rely on more than the woman's natural cycles. The Pill and condoms

People today can choose how many children to have and the age gaps between them, by using birth control

are examples of artificial methods of contraception. 'Natural' methods of contraception are allowed. These are methods where the couple have sex at a time of the month when the woman is not likely to get pregnant.

Roman Catholics believe that God made sex so that married people could have children. They believe that people should have sex for the right reasons. Roman Catholics believe that sex is spoiled if it is not between married people, or if there is no chance that a baby might be started. Natural methods of contraception do not always stop a woman becoming pregnant, so there is always the chance of a baby if this is what God plans.

In 1968, the Pope made a statement called 'On Human Life'. In this statement, he told Roman Catholics that they should use only natural methods of contraception.

THE TEACHING OF OTHER CHRISTIAN CHURCHES

Other Christian Churches, such as the Church of England, do not agree with the Roman Catholics about contraception. They say that adults should be responsible for how many children they have. They say that it is sensible for people to use contraception, because it is better if all children are wanted, and better if parents can choose not to have more children than they can afford to look after.

Some churches teach that it is sensible to limit the size of a family

FERTILITY TREATMENT AND THE 'RIGHT TO A CHILD'

If people want to have a baby but the woman does not get pregnant, they might use fertility treatment. Sometimes, people want fertility treatment because they are in a homosexual relationship, or they do not have a partner, or they are too old to have children without medical help.

There are different kinds of fertility treatment. Sometimes, drugs can be used to cure the problem. Often it is quite hard to find a method that works. Some people have to wait months or even years for a baby, and fertility treatment does not work for everyone.

IVF is one method of fertility treatment. It stands for **in vitro fertilisation**, which means that the egg is fertilised 'in vitro' or 'in glass'. The egg and sperm are brought together in a test tube, and if an embryo is formed, it is carefully put back inside the woman's body to grow into a baby.

Artificial Insemination is another form of fertility treatment. This is when sperm is collected and placed inside the woman's body. Sometimes this is the husband's sperm (**AIH**, or Artificial Insemination by Husband), but if he cannot produce healthy sperm or the woman does not have a male partner, then sperm can be used from a donor. This is called **AID** (Artificial Insemination by Donor).

IVF and other forms of fertility treatment do not always work. They can cost a lot of money. But if they do work, people can become parents and this makes them very happy.

DIFFERENT OPINIONS

Some Christians think that fertility treatments such as IVF and AI are good, because they help people who cannot have children. They might say that life comes from God, so if something makes new life, it has to be good. In the Bible, Adam and Eve were told to have children, and Christians might think this means God wants everyone to have children. Christians might use the idea of **agape** (love), and think about how they would feel if they could not have the children they wanted. They might decide that it is loving to offer people fertility treatment, because it can make them happy.

Other Christians might think that fertility treatment is wrong. They might say that God chooses if people have babies or not. Perhaps God chooses that some people should not be parents. They might think it is not natural for babies to be made in other ways than by people having sex.

Most Christians think that the right answer is somewhere in between. They say that fertility treatment is often good, but it can sometimes be wrong.

IVF can cause problems of right and wrong, because when the doctors try to make a new embryo, they have to fertilise more than one egg, to try and make sure that at least one of them grows into a baby. This means that there can be embryos left over, that are 'spare'.

It is difficult to know what to do with these spare embryos. Sometimes, they are thrown away. Sometimes, they are frozen, and used later if the woman wants to get pregnant again. Sometimes, they are used for research, to help in experiments to find cures for serious illnesses.

Some people think it is wrong to treat embryos as 'spares'. They might think that human life begins as soon as an egg is fertilised,

BIRTH AND DEATH

so the embryos are human lives. They might think these embryos should not be thrown away, because it is the same as killing a human life.

Other people think that Artificial Insemination might be wrong in some cases. If sperm is used from a donor and not from the husband, some people think this is like adultery, because it brings a third adult into the relationship. Some people think it could cause problems for the child as it grows up.

People also think it could be wrong for people to have fertility treatment if they are too old to have babies naturally, or if they are homosexual. They might say that it is not natural, and not fair to the baby.

Many people say that people should think of babies as a gift from God. They should not act as though they have a right to have a baby. But other people say that doctors should help people who are having problems getting pregnant. They say it is just the same as helping people with other kinds of medical problems.

CHURCH TEACHING

Different Churches have different ideas about fertility treatment.

The **Roman Catholic Church** teaches that human embryos are human lives. It says that they must not be thrown away. It also teaches that Artificial Insemination is allowed if the sperm comes from the husband, but not if it comes from someone else.

The **Methodist Church** teaches that it can be right for doctors and scientists to use 'spare' embryos for research. This is because it could help people to find cures for serious illnesses. But the Church says that this research should only be allowed in the first fourteen days after the embryo is made.

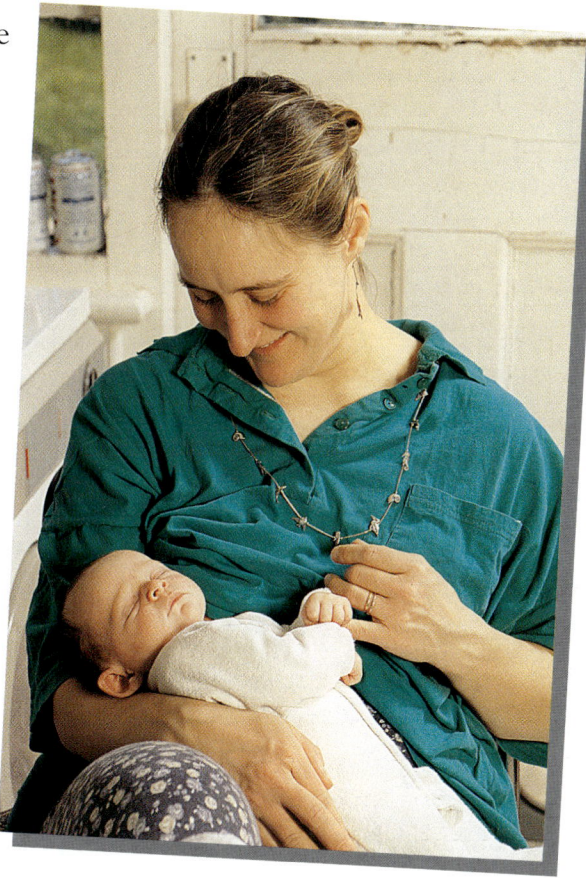

Fertility treatment can bring great happiness to people, but some Christians are worried about aspects of it

FOR DISCUSSION

Do you think that everyone who wants to have a baby should have the right to be given fertility treatment?

CHRISTIAN PERSPECTIVES

ABORTION

An abortion is when a foetus (unborn child) leaves its mother's body before it is ready to be born. If this happens naturally, it is often called a **miscarriage**. When people talk about abortion, they usually mean a **procured abortion**, which is when the pregnancy is deliberately ended.

Abortion usually happens early in the pregnancy, in the first three or four months. It is safer for the mother if it happens early, and she might not want other people to know that she was pregnant. Sometimes, abortions happen later. The law says that a pregnancy can only be ended deliberately in the first 24 weeks, because after this, if the baby is born it could survive.

There are many reasons why a woman might want an abortion, such as:

- She might not be in a relationship, and might not want to bring up the baby on her own.
- She might be pregnant at a time which does not suit her. For example, she might be a student or just about to start a new job, or she might already have older children and not want a new baby.
- The foetus might not be growing normally. If the baby is born, it might have serious health problems.
- She might be pregnant because she has been raped.
- Having the baby might make her ill.
- She might just not want to have a baby.

Some people think that a woman should be able to choose to have an abortion if she wants one. They think it is her body, and up to her to do what she wants if she is pregnant. People who think like this are called **pro-choice**. They do not like to be called pro-abortion, because they are not trying to say that there should be more abortions. They want women to have a free choice about what they do.

Other people think that if someone wants an abortion, it should be discussed with the father and with doctors. They think that some reasons for wanting an abortion are better than others. If a woman wants an abortion because the pregnancy would kill her, they would think that was a good reason. If a woman wanted an abortion because she just did not feel it was

FOR DISCUSSION

Do you think that some of these reasons for having an abortion are good reasons? Do you think some are bad reasons? Explain your answer.

the right time for a baby, they might think that was a bad reason.

The law says that a woman has to have a good reason before she can have an abortion. She has to get two doctors to agree that it would be best if she had an abortion. Doctors and nurses do not have to take part in doing abortions, if it is against their beliefs.

ABORTION AND THE SANCTITY OF LIFE

When people talk about abortion, they often think about whether a foetus is a person or not. Some Christians think that the foetus is a person, even though it has not yet been born as a baby. They think it still matters to God, and it still has rights. But others believe that the foetus is not yet a person. They sometimes say it is like an acorn and an oak tree – the acorn might become an oak tree, but it is not an oak tree yet. They say it would be wrong to kill a living child, but it might not always be wrong to end the life of a foetus.

If a woman wants to have an abortion, she has to explain her reasons to doctors

Roman Catholics believe that life begins as soon as an egg is fertilised. They think that from this moment, the life is sacred and matters to God. It is a human life like other human lives. Many Christians from other churches also agree with this view.

But other people think that a foetus cannot really be a person right from the start. They think it is just a group of cells. Some people think it becomes a person when the mother can first feel it move inside her, at about 14 weeks of pregnancy. Others think it is a person when it could survive if it was born, after about 22 weeks.

BIBLICAL TEACHING ABOUT ABORTION

There is not much teaching about abortion in the Bible. When the Bible was written, girls were married very young. Abortion was not safe, and there were not tests to tell whether the baby would be healthy, so abortion did not happen as often as it does today.

But many Christians use teachings from the Bible to support their views about abortion.

Some point out that the Bible talks about the **sanctity of life** (see page 30). They say that the Bible teaches that people are made 'in the image of God' (Genesis 1: 26). They show that the Bible says murder is wrong (Exodus 20: 13).

Christians might use the book of Jeremiah when they are talking about abortion or contraception. God told Jeremiah:

> *Before I formed you in the womb I knew you, before you were born I set you apart; I appointed you as a prophet to the nations.*
>
> (Jeremiah 1: 5)

People might use this verse to show that God knows and plans every person even before he or she is born. They might say it shows that it would be wrong to stop a life being born, by using contraception or abortion, because it would spoil God's plan.

One passage in the Bible is about what should happen if someone hurts a pregnant woman and she loses the baby:

> *If men who are fighting hit a pregnant woman and she gives birth prematurely but there is no serious injury,* **the offender must be fined** *whatever the woman's husband demands and the court allows. But if there is serious injury, you are to take life for life, eye for eye, tooth for tooth, hand for hand, foot for foot, burn for burn, wound for wound, bruise for bruise.*
>
> (Exodus 21: 22–25)

This passage seems to be saying that killing an unborn child is not as serious as other kinds of killing.

CHURCH TEACHING ABOUT ABORTION

Different Churches have different views about abortion. The Roman Catholic Church teaches that it is always wrong to kill an unborn child. It says the foetus is a human life and is sacred. It should be treated like any other human being. The Roman Catholic Church says that abortion should not happen even if the woman has been raped, because the foetus should not be killed for someone else's crime. Roman Catholics often try to stop women having abortions, and get them to think about having the baby adopted instead.

The Roman Catholic Church has made several statements about abortion. It said that human life is sacred, and all people should respect it.

Other Churches think that abortion is not

BIRTH AND DEATH

always wrong. The Salvation Army teaches that it could be the right thing to do if the mother might die unless she has an abortion. It could also be right if the baby is going to be very ill and will not live long. The United Reformed Church says that it makes a difference if the woman is only just pregnant or if the foetus has been growing for several weeks.

All the Christian Churches teach that women who want abortions need plenty of care and help.

CHRISTIAN BELIEFS IN ACTION

There are many things Christians might do if they have beliefs that abortion is wrong. For example:

- If they are talking about abortion with other people, they might explain why they think it is wrong, and tell them about their Christian beliefs.
- A Christian might join a group that speaks out against abortion, such as Life or SPUC (Society for the Protection of the Unborn Child).
- They might use their vote for an MP who promises to make abortion more difficult.
- They might take part in protests against abortion. For example, they might write letters or go on marches.
- They might pray about abortion, asking God to help people not to choose it.
- They might try to help with sex education for young people, to teach them how to avoid getting pregnant before they are ready.
- Some Christians think that it is not enough, just to stop people having abortions. These people have to be helped, too. So Christians might offer people support if they have a disabled child, or if they are single parents. Some Christians offer to babysit, or they might foster children whose parents are not able to look after them all the time.
- Christians might think that it is better to have a baby adopted than to have an abortion. A Christian might help someone who was pregnant to have the baby adopted into a loving home.

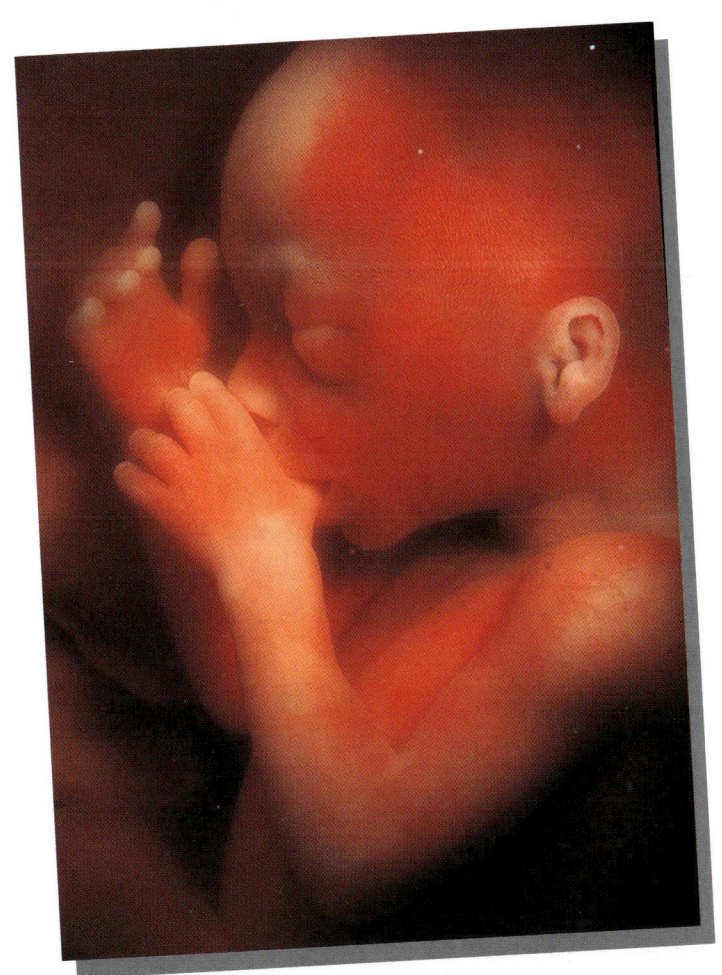

Some Christians believe that abortion is the same as murder, even though the child has not yet been born

CHRISTIAN PERSPECTIVES

If Christians agree that women should be able to choose to have abortions, they could put their beliefs into action, too:

- They might join a group that works to give people the right to choose abortion.
- They might support a group that gives help and advice to people who have had abortions.
- They might explain their views when people are talking about abortion. They might say why they think it is sometimes the most loving thing to do. They might stop other people from being too hard on women who have chosen to have abortions.
- They might pray about the problem of abortion.
- Even if they think abortion can sometimes be the best choice, Christians might help to give young people a better sex education to stop them needing abortions.

THE 1967 ABORTION ACT

Before 1967, abortion was against the law. If a woman wanted an abortion, she had to try and find someone who would do it in secret. Sometimes, these people had no proper training, and they could not use a proper hospital. Many women were badly hurt as a result of these 'back-street abortions' and some died. The 1967 Abortion Act made it much easier for women to have safe abortions. If two doctors agreed that the woman needed an abortion, then she could have one safely with proper medical care.

SPUC – AN ORGANISATION WHICH CAMPAIGNS AGAINST ABORTION

A lot of people thought it was very wrong to make a law allowing abortion. They thought it was allowing murder, and they said it stopped women looking at other things they might do, such as having the baby adopted. Some of these people joined together in 1967 and formed a group called the Society for the Protection of the Unborn Child, or SPUC.

SPUC is not a Christian group. But Christians might choose to support it, because the work of SPUC might fit in with their Christian beliefs. SPUC tries to tell other people that abortion is wrong. It also believes that euthanasia and embryo experiments are wrong. SPUC says that since the law allowed abortions, over 4.5 million pregnancies have been ended. SPUC members believe that human life begins as soon as the egg is fertilised, and they believe that an unborn child has a right to life. They think that it is wrong to have an abortion if the baby will be born disabled, because they believe that disabled people have just as much right to life as anyone else.

Members of SPUC raise money to spend on advertising their point of view. They have street marches, especially when people try to change the law to make abortion easier. They write to MPs and try to get them to vote against abortion. They make booklets and videos for schools to use, to explain to young people what abortion is about and why they think it is wrong.

Christians might support SPUC because of their belief that life is sacred. They might think it is wrong to do nothing to stop abortion. The Bible teaches that it is important to look after the weak:

> *Rescue the weak and needy; deliver them from the hand of the wicked.*
>
> (Psalm 82: 4)

They might think that joining a group such as SPUC is the best way of putting their faith into action.

THE ALL-PARTY PARLIAMENTARY PRO-CHOICE GROUP

The All-Party Parliamentary Pro-Choice Group is also called the Pro-Choice Alliance (PCA). This is a group that thinks women should have the right to choose abortion. The members think women should not have to explain to doctors their reasons for wanting an abortion. They try to change the law to make abortion easier.

The PCA thinks that women should be able to make their own choices. If women have to tell doctors why they want an abortion, and then the doctor agrees or disagrees, the PCA says it is treating women as if they were children. It is not allowing women to be private and make up their own minds.

Some Christians might support the work of the PCA. They might use passages from the Bible that show that men and women have equal value (see page 69) to show that women should be able to make choices about their own lives. Christians might think it is loving and forgiving to allow a woman to choose to have an abortion, rather than making her go through with a pregnancy she does not want.

CHRISTIAN PERSPECTIVES

People often have strong feelings about abortion. Some Christians take part in protests about abortion

IN YOUR NOTES

What is your own opinion about abortion? Give reasons to support your answer.

SUICIDE

Suicide is when a person ends his or her own life. It is not very common. In the UK, fewer than one in every hundred deaths are because of suicide. But it happens often enough to affect many families. About three times more men than women commit suicide. The suicide rate among young people is rising.

There are many different reasons why someone might commit suicide.

- Mental illness sometimes makes people feel they have no hope for the future.
- Drink, drugs and money problems can make people feel there is no way out except suicide.
- Sometimes, people feel there is no point in carrying on living when someone they love dies.
- Bullying can make some people feel like committing suicide.
- When people are old and are not able to look after themselves, they sometimes feel life is not worth living any more.

BIRTH AND DEATH

- If someone has a serious and painful illness that will kill them slowly, they might want to die quickly instead.
- Some people commit suicide because they are under pressure and they feel that they are letting everyone down.

Sometimes, people try to commit suicide, but they hope someone will find them before they die. This is often called a 'cry for help'. They hope someone will see how unhappy they are, and will help them sort out their problems.

In the past, people thought suicide was a bad crime. The Church thought it was a sin. People who tried and failed to commit suicide were punished. People who did take their own lives were not allowed to be buried on church ground, but had graves away from everyone else.

Today, people understand a lot more about suicide. They understand mental illness, and how people feel when someone dies. Today, people try to offer help and support instead of punishment.

Most Christians think it is wrong to commit suicide, but they know that people who try to do it are often too upset to think sensibly. Christians might argue against suicide by saying:

- God chooses the right time for us to be born and to die. We should not think we know better.
- Many Christians say suffering brings them closer to God. It helps them understand the suffering of Jesus. They say God can teach people things through suffering. If someone commits suicide, they are not learning the things God wants to teach them.
- Suicide is selfish and hurts the people left behind. It can be very hard to cope with the death of someone who has committed suicide. The people left behind feel guilty and think they should have been able to stop it.
- One of the Ten Commandments is 'Do not murder'. Christians might believe that suicide is a kind of murder, even if the murderer and the victim are the same person.

For all sorts of reasons people sometimes feel that they can no longer cope with life

The most famous example of suicide in the Bible was that of Judas, after he betrayed Jesus. Judas led the soldiers to Jesus, and they paid him 30 pieces of silver. Judas felt so bad about this that he hanged himself. The Bible does not say whether Judas was right or wrong to do this.

When Paul wrote letters to the new Christian churches, he said that Christians should look after their bodies. He said they should think of their bodies as being like temples, where God lives. They should respect their bodies and not harm them (1 Corinthians 3: 16).

Most Christians believe that it is right to be loving and forgiving to someone who wants to commit suicide.

THE SAMARITANS

The Samaritans is a group that Christians might want to support. It was started by a Christian, but anyone can use it. They do not have to be religious. The aim of The Samaritans is to prevent suicide. They try to support people who need help, so that they feel they can carry on living. They also try to help everyone understand more about suicide, so that they can help each other.

The Samaritans was started in 1953 by a vicar called Chad Varah. He was working for the Church of England in London. One of the first jobs he had to do when he started working as a vicar was a funeral for a 14-year-old girl. She had killed herself. It was because she had started her periods, and did not know what was happening to her. She thought she had a disease, and did not feel she could talk to anyone about it.

Chad Varah was very upset by this. He wanted to start a group where people could talk about their problems. He thought it was important that they could talk to someone they did not know, and that they did not have to give their names. There had to be people who were ready to listen day and night, every day of the year, including Christmas.

BIRTH AND DEATH

FOR DISCUSSION

Why do you think suicide is so much more common among men than women?

Christians might support the work of a group such as The Samaritans. They might think it fits in with Christian beliefs

The Samaritans has people who volunteer to listen on the telephone or answer e-mails. They work for a few hours every month. The telephone number is on posters, stickers and leaflets in public places. Anyone with a problem can call the number and talk to someone who will listen.

The volunteers should not tell the callers what to do about their problems. They listen, and help the callers to work out their own answers. The volunteers can come from any background and any religion. They are not allowed to give their own opinions or beliefs to the callers.

Today, there are branches of The Samaritans all over the country, and in other countries, too. There are places where people can call in and talk about their problems face to face. If people want to e-mail someone about their problems, there are volunteers to answer them. There are still the telephone lines. If the people who worked for The Samaritans had to be paid, instead of doing it for nothing, it would cost more than £10 million a year.

ICT FOR RESEARCH

Visit The Samaritans' web-site:
http://www.samaritans.org

IN YOUR NOTES

Answer the following questions:
(a) What do people who volunteer to work for The Samaritans have to do?
(b) Why do you think the volunteers are not allowed to tell the callers about their own opinions and beliefs?

CHRISTIAN PERSPECTIVES

EUTHANASIA

The word 'euthanasia' means 'a good death'.

When people talk about euthanasia, they mean making the choice about how death happens. It is like suicide in some ways, because it is about choosing when a life is worth living. But the difference between euthanasia and suicide is that suicide only takes one person. Euthanasia takes more than one person – there is the one who is dying, and the one who does the killing.

Voluntary euthanasia is when someone wants to end his or her own life, but is not able to do it without help. This is often called 'assisted suicide'.

Involuntary euthanasia is when other people decide that someone's life should end, because that person is not able to choose. The person might be in a coma, or might be only a few hours old.

Active euthanasia is when something is done to end someone's life; for example, if someone is given an injection to kill them. This is against the law.

Passive euthanasia is when nothing is done to save someone's life, and treatment is stopped, to make death come more quickly. This happens quite often.

Euthanasia is an issue today because doctors now have many ways of keeping people alive in intensive care. People might be badly hurt in accidents, and they might be brain damaged so that they will never wake up, but they can still be kept alive. Euthanasia is not just about killing. It is also about deciding whether to keep someone alive. Sometimes, it can seem more sensible not to keep someone alive when they will never get any better.

People often think about euthanasia if they have a serious illness, when it gives them a lot of pain and there is no cure. They might not want to carry on in pain for a long time, getting worse and worse. They might want to say goodbye to their family and friends, and then die quickly.

One of the main things to think about is a person's **quality of life**. If someone has a happy life, they are not in too much pain, and they can talk to their friends and family, then most people would agree that euthanasia would be wrong. But if someone is

---

FOR DISCUSSION

What does the phrase 'a good death' mean to you? If you could choose how and when to die, what would you choose, and why?

BIRTH AND DEATH

in pain and is not able to enjoy life, then it might seem as though euthanasia is the best choice.

THE DEBATE ABOUT EUTHANASIA

Some people believe euthanasia should not be against the law. They say that if people are well, they can choose to commit suicide, so if people are not well enough to commit suicide on their own, they should be allowed to have help with it. They say it is cruel to make someone carry on living if they are in pain. Most people would have their pets put down, if they were in a lot of pain and were not going to get better. So some people think we should be able to do this for people, too.

The Voluntary Euthanasia Society works to change the law, so that people can choose euthanasia without anyone being taken to court. They would like people to be able to put their wishes in writing, in case they get to a point when they cannot speak for themselves but want to be allowed to die.

Some Christians agree with this point of view. They say that the main thing is to think about how you would feel, if you

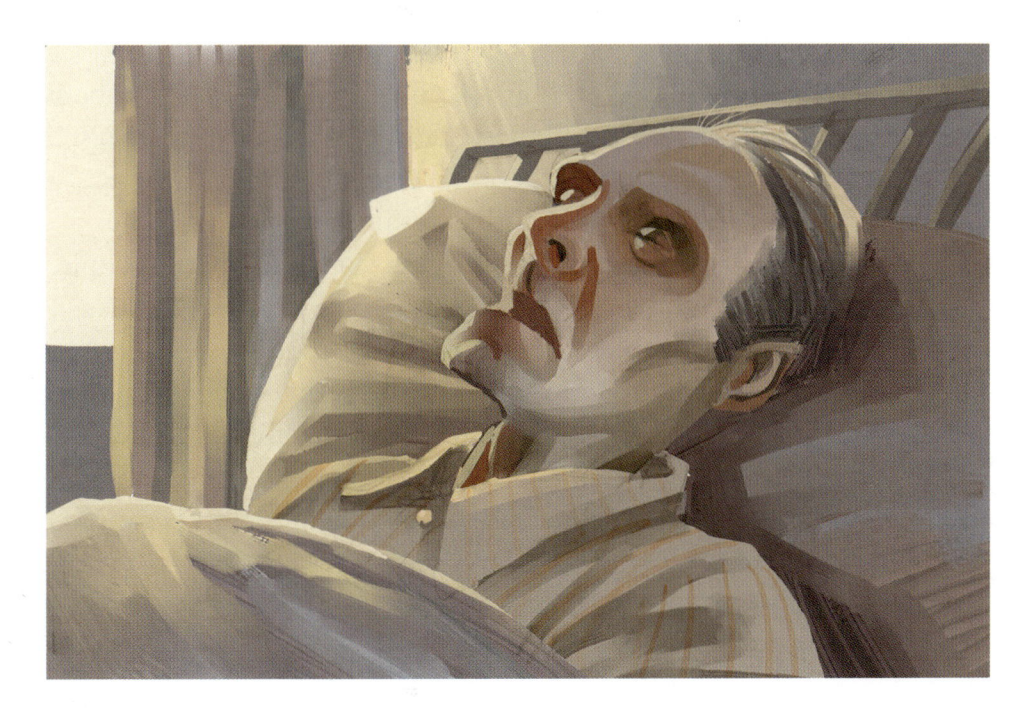

When people are thinking about euthanasia, the quality of someone's life is often important

47

CHRISTIAN PERSPECTIVES

were the person who was in pain. You should treat others in the way that you would like to be treated, and put the principle of agape into practice.

Other people think it would be wrong to make a law allowing euthanasia. They think people might be pushed into saying they wanted euthanasia, by family who did not want to look after them or who wanted their money. People who are in pain do not always make sensible choices. They might change their minds about euthanasia, and not be able to tell anyone. Many Christians agree with this point of view. They also say that it is wrong to take away human life, because it is sacred.

CHURCH TEACHING ABOUT EUTHANASIA

The **Baptist Church** teaches that euthanasia, like abortion, raises problems of whether it is right to take away human life. Most Baptists are against euthanasia. They believe all human life is sacred, so they think it should be cared for. But Baptists usually agree that if someone is in a coma and doctors agree that they will never get any better, then it would be all right for the patient to be allowed to die. They do not agree in doing things like giving lethal injections.

The **Church of England** has taken part in a lot of talks about euthanasia. It agrees that human life is sacred. But it also says that doctors do not have to do everything to keep someone alive, when their lives are clearly painful and unhappy. The Church also says that it is important to make old and ill people feel they are wanted.

The **Roman Catholic Church** is against euthanasia. It says that doing anything to help someone die is the same as murder. It teaches that ordinary ways of keeping someone alive, such as feeding, must not be stopped. But doctors do not have to do everything to keep someone alive, such as a difficult operation that is not likely to work anyway.

> **IN YOUR NOTES**
>
> Give some examples of Biblical teaching which Christians might use in a discussion about euthanasia. You could choose passages which talk about agape, or the Golden Rule (Matthew 7: 12), or the sanctity of life.

BIRTH AND DEATH

THE HOSPICE MOVEMENT

In the past, a hospice was a place where people could go for care, if they were travellers, or ill, or old, or homeless.

Today, a hospice is a place for people who are terminally ill. 'Terminally ill' means ill with something that cannot be cured and will cause death. Hospices also help the family and friends of people who are terminally ill. They give pain relief to the person who is ill, and they try to make them more comfortable in all kinds of ways. They help them with more minor health problems, such as sore skin. They help them to sort out money problems and to say goodbye to people. Hospices try to give people a good death, so that they do not need euthanasia.

Modern hospices first began when a group of nuns from Dublin set up a home for the dying. This was in the nineteenth century (1800s). The work spread to London. A young nurse called Cicely Saunders spent many years working in St Joseph's Hospice, and then she set up St Christopher's Hospice in 1967.

Hospice work in the UK was begun by people with Christian faith. They believed it was important for people who are dying to be able to face death in a good way. But hospices are not just for Christians, and not everyone who works there is a Christian. The staff do not try to make people believe in God, but people can see priests or ministers if this is what they want.

ICT FOR RESEARCH

Many UK hospices have websites, where you can find out more about the staff, the volunteers, and the work that they do. Try one of the following:

http://www.derianhouse.org.uk
http://www.boltonhospice.org
http://freespace.virgin.net/graham.leng/hospice

IN YOUR NOTES

Write a paragraph about one of the hospices you have explored, explaining what it is trying to achieve, the sorts of people it has as patients, and the different kinds of help it offers.

Hospices try to be like homes. They help dying patients and their families

CHRISTIAN PERSPECTIVES

Some hospices are just for children who are dying. They are places designed for children, with play areas, gardens and places for their parents, brothers and sisters to stay.

Not everyone goes to a hospice to die. Sometimes, hospices are used for 'respite care'. This means the patients just go there for a short while, to give the people who usually look after them a break. Many patients spend time in a hospice until death is very near, and then they go home to spend their last few days at home. Staff from the hospice go with them, to look after them. It is important that people can choose where they want to die, and do what feels best for them.

Special nurses, called Macmillan nurses, often visit patients at a hospice and in their homes. These nurses are trained to look after people who are terminally ill. They make sure the patient sees the same nurse each time, not always a different one when shifts change.

The hospice helps the family, as well as the patient. Family members often need someone to talk to. Even after the patient has died, the hospice carries on giving help to the family.

Some people work in hospices or as Macmillan nurses, because of their Christian faith. Other Christians support the hospices in other ways, such as by fund-raising, or working in a hospice charity shop.

Macmillan nurses provide support and care for people who are terminally ill

BIRTH AND DEATH

PRACTICE EXAMINATION QUESTIONS

1 (a) Describe Biblical teaching about the sanctity of life. (8 marks)

Remember that 'sanctity of life' is the belief that human life is holy, a gift from God, and different from other kinds of life. Notice that the question asks about Biblical teaching. This means you need to explain what the Bible says about life being holy. You need to say what the teaching is, in your own words. Try to use several different examples.

(b) Explain why Christians might support the work of an organisation that tries to prevent suicide. (7 marks)

Notice that the question asks about why a Christian might support this organisation. Your answer should show how the aims of the organisation fit in with Christian beliefs (about life being sacred, people being valuable to God, and so on). You can say something about what the organisation does, but remember to relate it to Christianity, because this is what the question asks.

(c) 'If people want to take their own lives, they should be free to do so.' Do you agree? Give reasons to support your answer, and show that you have thought about different points of view. You must refer to Christianity in your answer. (5 marks)

Remember that for full marks, you need to include a Christian view, another view, and your own view. Each time, you should try to give reasons for these opinions.

2 (a) Describe Christian teaching that might be used in a discussion about abortion. (8 marks)

Notice how the question asks for Christian teaching. This means you can use teaching from the Bible, from the Churches, or any other teaching that comes from Christians. You might want to show that you know different Churches have different teachings about abortion. You could include the views of the Roman Catholic Church, and the views of a different Church.

(b) Explain how a Christian might respond to someone who asked for euthanasia to end a painful illness. (7 marks)

Remember that Christians will have different opinions about this. Try and include the reasons why a Christian might give that answer. You could say something about how some Christians will think the sanctity of life is the most important thing. But other Christians might think it is more important to be loving.

(c) 'Doctors should preserve life in all circumstances.' Do you agree? Give reasons to support your answer, and show that you have thought about different points of view. You must refer to Christianity in your answer. (5 marks)

Do you think that doctors should always keep someone alive, no matter how old they are, or how badly disabled? Or do you think that sometimes doctors should allow people to die, because it is kinder? You might have strong views about this. But remember to include what a Christian might say, as well, and give reasons to explain these views.

4

PREJUDICE AND EQUALITY

**Christian understandings of issues concerning race and gender.
The work of one or more well-known Christians who have worked to overcome prejudice and discrimination.**

Prejudice means 'judging before'. We often do this; we make up our minds about something before we have found out much about it. For example, we might decide not to see a film because of the title. Sometimes, this does not matter. It does not matter much if we walk past a shop without going inside because we do not like the window display. But some kinds of prejudice are very serious. It matters if we make up our minds about other people just because of the way they look.

Many different kinds of people suffer from prejudice. People who are disabled, or who have learning difficulties, are often treated as if they have no feelings. Old people are often treated as though they have nothing to offer. Some people are prejudiced against homosexuals. People make up their minds about others before they know the facts.

Two serious forms of prejudice are racial prejudice and sexism.

RACIAL PREJUDICE

People who are racially prejudiced believe that people from some ethnic groups are better than people from others. They think they can judge someone just because of the colour of their skin or the country they come from.

Racial prejudice is also known as racism.

There are several reasons why people might be racist:

FOR DISCUSSION

Think of some of the ways that people who are racist judge Jews, Asians, the Irish, gypsies or black people.

- They might have been brought up by racist parents. Very young children are not racist. They notice if their friends have different colour hair or skin, but they do not judge them because of it. Racism is copied from other people.
- Racism sometimes comes from fear. People are afraid of things they do not know much about. If they meet people with different customs or a different language, they might be afraid. They might try to make themselves feel more powerful by picking on the people who are different. Racism is a form of bullying.
- Sometimes, there is a lot of racism in areas that are poor and

PREJUDICE AND EQUALITY

Today, in many towns, people of different races live and work together. Some people are afraid of this

where there are not many jobs. People look for someone to blame. They tell themselves the area would be better if some groups of people did not live there. Before the Second World War, the Germans blamed the Jews because the country did not have enough money. Today, people sometimes blame black or Asian people for things that go wrong.

Racial discrimination is when people put racism into action. If they believe some ethnic groups are not worth as much as others, they might try to give them worse houses, or an education which is not as good, or fewer jobs. Sometimes, racism leads to attacks, when people are hurt because of their ethnic group. 'Ethnic cleansing' is when racists have tried to wipe out an entire ethnic group.

Racial discrimination is against the law in the UK:

- It is against the law to use racist language or threats. People who do this can be given fines or even prison sentences.

CHRISTIAN PERSPECTIVES

Racism can lead to terrible results. Muslims were killed because of their race, in the former Yugoslavia

- It is against the law to give out letters or booklets that are trying to make people racist.
- It is against the law to turn someone down for a job just because of their race. It is also against the law to use race as a reason for not giving someone training or promotion.
- It is against the law to refuse to sell or rent a house to someone because of their race. The price has to be the same for everyone. Hotels, swimming pools, restaurants, pubs, cinemas and all sorts of other public places are not allowed to treat one ethnic group in a different way from others.

The Commission for Racial Equality is run by the government. It takes people to court if they break the laws about racism.

There is still racial discrimination in the UK. Many people suffer abuse, and have worse jobs and housing, just because of their race.

RACISM IN HISTORY

There has always been prejudice against people because of their race. When one race moves into another country, there are often bad feelings between the two groups. For example, four thousand years ago, the Indus Valley in India was taken over by people known as Aryans. They were a different race from the people who already lived in the Indus Valley. They wrote racist things about the Indus Valley people, and said they were ugly, snub-nosed, and not as good as Aryan people. In England at the time of Shakespeare, there was racism against the Jews. It is not anything new.

PREJUDICE AND EQUALITY

Racism has always been a way in which some people have tried to get power over others. They use it as an excuse to be greedy. They want more than their fair share, so they say that other people are not worth as much as they are, and do not deserve or need fair treatment.

The **slave trade** was important in the history of racism. During the slave trade, which ended about two hundred years ago, black people were taken away from their homes to be sold as slaves. They were packed onto ships in a way that is against the law today, even for cattle. They were sold as slaves to white families. Their owners could work them as hard as they wanted to, and often beat them. If the owners wanted to sell one of them, they might split up the slave family and they would never see each other again. Some of the slave owners were members of the Christian Church. They said that black people were not really human, and Christian teaching about care for others did not include black people. The slave trade ended when it started costing too much money. The black people were free, but they had to live in countries where they had no money and no power.

In the past, people from Europe ruled in countries such as India. They did not see anything wrong with this

CHRISTIAN PERSPECTIVES

Colonialism was also important in the history of racism. People from Europe, such as the French, the Dutch, the English and the Germans tried to get more power by going to other countries and taking them over. They put their own governments in power, and kept the best places and the most money for themselves. They tried to change the customs of the people who lived there. They made them eat with knives and forks, wear Western clothes, and change from their own religions to Christianity.

The people of Europe also took diseases with them when they went to other countries. These diseases often killed many people. For example, many North American Indians died of smallpox after the British and the French took the disease to their country.

Children in Europe were taught to feel proud of the Empire. They were told that it was a good thing for people in other countries to learn to be more like Europeans.

THE EFFECTS OF HISTORY ON RACISM TODAY

Slavery and colonialism still affect people today. The slave trade is over, but in the 1960s black people were asked to come to the UK, because there were not enough workers. The black people were given the jobs that no one else wanted to do. They swept the roads and worked the night shifts on London Transport. They were given the worst houses and the lowest wages.

Then in the 1970s, when there were not as many jobs for everyone, white people decided there were too many black people in the country. They wanted to send the black people back to the countries they came from, even if they had been in the UK for many years. People seemed to think that they could use black people when they needed them for work, and get rid of them when they wanted to.

Colonialism has made some of the problems in the Developing World. When white people went to some of these countries, they took away money, which has never been given back. World trade in gold, oil, diamonds and other important goods is still run mainly by white people, even though these things are found in countries where most people are black. The media gives people the idea that black people are poor and need white people to help them. But it does not often say that white people have done a lot to make black people poor in the first place.

Black people were asked to come to the UK when there were not enough workers

APARTHEID IN SOUTH AFRICA

South Africa had a racist government in the twentieth century. It began in 1948, and it was called **apartheid.**

The government made laws to keep white and black people apart. More than 70% of the people in South Africa are black, and fewer than 20% are white. But the white people had more than their fair share of everything. They took most of the land for themselves. The black people had to live in crowded areas called 'homelands'. Black people had bad houses, health care and education. They were not allowed out of the homelands without a special pass. To find work, they often had to live a long way away from their families. Black people could be held by the police without a trial, for up to three months. They were often beaten by the police, and sometimes killed.

People were not allowed to protest against apartheid. When some people tried to hold a protest in a town called Sharpeville in 1960, many of them were killed or injured. In 1976, black people in Soweto began to riot, and 400 were killed.

It was against the law to protest against apartheid, but many brave people broke the law. Nelson Mandela was one of them. He worked to fight apartheid, and was sent to prison in 1964. Steve Biko was another man who tried to do something to stop apartheid, after the people were killed in Soweto. He was arrested, and died while he was being held by the police.

It was dangerous to try to do anything about apartheid, but people did not give up. In 1990, Nelson Mandela was set free from prison. He had been there 26 years. Apartheid was finished. In 1994, Nelson Mandela became

Nelson Mandela was put in prison for 26 years for fighting apartheid in South Africa

President of South Africa.

Some of the people who worked against apartheid were Christians. They thought apartheid was wrong, because of their Christian beliefs.

CHRISTIAN PERSPECTIVES

TREVOR HUDDLESTON

Trevor Huddleston was a white man who came from a well-off family in London. He remembered something that happened when he was a child:

I can remember a strange little incident, which I suppose is revealing. When I was about 12 or 13 and my father was home and we had our own house in Hampstead Garden Suburb or just near it, one evening around Christmas – the night was quite cold and dark – the bell rang and I saw an old Indian looking in through the glass pane. I opened the door and my father than came out and he said – not roughly, because he wasn't that kind of a person – 'No, there's nothing here for you.' I remember that incident to this day. It seemed to me a terrible thing, not only because he was black but because he was poor, and I couldn't believe that at Christmas time you could turn anybody away.

Trevor Huddleston put his Christian beliefs into action by fighting apartheid

As he grew up, he learned more about the problems of the poor in the UK. His school did some work for the poor, and Trevor realised that some children in London had no shoes and not enough to eat.

When he left Oxford University, Trevor decided to become a priest. He wanted to put his Christian faith into action and do something to help the poor. He wanted to make the world a fairer place.

In 1943, Trevor was sent by his church to work in South Africa. He went to Sophiatown, a poor area for black people. He had a church to look after, and also he had to try and improve education for the black children. He worked to get more money for their schools, and to get free school meals for the poorest children. One boy of 13 was ill in hospital for two years, and Trevor visited him and took books for him. The boy was Desmond Tutu. They were friends for the rest of Trevor's life.

In 1948, South Africa began the apartheid system, to keep black people and white people apart. Trevor had been in South Africa for five years by then. He had to try and put his Christian beliefs into action in a country where black people were not treated fairly. He thought that it was his duty as a Christian to fight against apartheid.

Trevor Huddleston became friends with other people who were fighting apartheid. Sophiatown was knocked down, and all the people had to find somewhere else to live. He spoke out and said this was unfair. The government of South Africa had him watched. They wanted to catch him breaking the law so that they could arrest him.

One of the ways Trevor Huddleston worked against apartheid was by organising boycotts. (A boycott is when people refuse to deal with a country or a company, because they want to

PREJUDICE AND EQUALITY

show they do not agree with what it does.) He thought of getting countries around the world to refuse to have anything to do with South Africa. Then South Africa would have to change its rules if it wanted to carry on trading and making money. The sports boycott worked very well. Teams from all over the world would not play sports, such as football and cricket, against South African teams. The white South Africans hated this because sport is a big part of South African life.

Bands refused to give concerts in South Africa. Families in the UK and in other countries would not buy South African goods, such as apples, when they did their shopping. This all helped to bring an end to apartheid. Trevor Huddleston talked to Margaret Thatcher, who was the Prime Minister, about getting the UK to stop trading with South Africa, but she would not agree with him.

Trevor Huddleston became one of the leaders of the Anti-Apartheid Movement. He became a close friend of many others who worked against apartheid, such as Nelson Mandela, Oliver Tambo and Archbishop Desmond Tutu.

People would not play sports with South African teams, to show that they did not agree with apartheid

Some people said that Father Trevor Huddleston should not take part in politics. They said that because he was a priest, he should spend his time doing religious things, like choosing hymns and writing sermons. But he believed that working to make the world a fairer place is part of what it means to be a Christian. He believed that all people are equal in the way they matter to God. He worked for justice all his life. He lived long enough to see Nelson Mandela walk out of prison after 26 years, and he saw apartheid come to an end. Trevor Huddleston died on 20 April 1998.

FOR DISCUSSION

Do you think priests should keep out of politics?

Trevor Huddleston believed that fighting against injustice is an important part of being a Christian. (On the left is George Carey, former Archbishop of Canterbury, and on the right, Desmond Tutu.)

59

CHRISTIAN PERSPECTIVES

MARTIN LUTHER KING JNR

In the past, black people were stolen from their homes in Africa, and taken to America to work as slaves for white people. In 1869, Abraham Lincoln, who was President of the USA, made a law to stop slavery. But the black people who were set free found life in the USA very difficult. Most white people thought that they were better than black people. The black people had very little money. White people did not want to give black people fair pay for their work, and they did not want to be employed by black people. They did not want their children to go to the same schools, and they did not want to eat in the same restaurants or let black people have a vote.

Martin Luther King Jnr was born in the USA in 1929. Racism was part of normal life. He was the son of a black Christian minister in the state of Georgia. At home and at church, he learned that God made everyone in his own image. He learned that Jesus cared for all people. But when he went out, he saw how his family and other black people were treated badly because of their colour. It made him angry, but he wanted to try and change things using peace, not violence. He did not want to become as bad as the Ku Klux Klan, who attacked black people. He tried to put into practice the teaching of Jesus:

Before the Civil Rights Movement, black people were not treated as well as white people

ICT FOR RESEARCH

Visit the web-site:
www.wmich.edu/politics/mlk
Find out more about the work of the Civil Rights Movement in the USA.

You have heard that it was said, 'Eye for eye, and tooth for tooth.' But I tell you, Do not resist an evil person. If someone strikes you on the right cheek, turn to him the other also. (Matthew 5: 38–9)

When he grew up, Martin Luther King became a Baptist minister. He lived in Montgomery, Alabama. In Montgomery, there was a rule that black people could sit only at the back of a bus, not at the front. The front seats were for white people. If a white person wanted to sit where a black person was sitting, the black person had to get out of the seat.

In 1955, a black woman called Rosa Parks sat down on a bus on her way home from work. A white man got on the bus, and wanted her seat, so he told her to get up. She refused. The driver would not drive on, and the police were called. Rosa was

FOR DISCUSSION

Do you think that Martin Luther King would have achieved more if he had used violence?

PREJUDICE AND EQUALITY

arrested and taken to jail. She had many black friends who wanted to help her, because they too thought the rules were not fair. The next day, 50 black leaders had a meeting at the church where Martin Luther King was minister. They decided that the black people should all work together and refuse to go on the buses at all, until the rule changed. The bus companies soon began to lose money. A lot of their customers were black – white people often travelled by car. The rule was changed, so that black people could sit where they wanted to on the buses. This was the beginning of the American Civil Rights Movement. Martin Luther King was its leader.

Martin Luther King believed that it could never be right to use violence against racism. People bombed his house and said they would kill his children, but he stuck to his Christian beliefs. He said hate must be faced with love. He organised boycotts and marches, and he gave speeches to huge crowds. He told people about his dreams for the future of the USA. His most famous speech was made on the steps of the memorial to Abraham Lincoln in Washington DC, in August 1963:

I have a dream that one day this nation will rise up and live out the true meaning of its creed: 'We hold these truths to be self-evident: that all men are created equal.'

I have a dream that my four children will one day live in a nation where they will not be judged by the colour of their skin but by the content of their character.

I have a dream today.

In 1968, when he was only 39, Martin Luther King Jnr was shot dead. The Civil Rights Movement went on.

Martin Luther King's speeches drew large crowds. He preached a message of Christian non-violence

IN YOUR NOTES

(a) Why do you think Martin Luther King chose the Lincoln Memorial as the place to give his speech? (Clue: what change did Lincoln make in the law about slavery?)

(b) Martin Luther King worked against racism because he was a Christian. Why do Christians believe racism is wrong?

CHRISTIAN TEACHING ABOUT PREJUDICE

The Bible says quite clearly that people should treat each other as equals. But Christians have not always followed this teaching.

In the Old Testament, for example, the laws tell people how to treat people from other countries (called 'aliens' here):

> When an alien lives with you in your land, **do not ill-treat him**. The alien living with you must be treated as one of your native-born. **Love him as yourself**, for you were aliens in Egypt. I am the LORD your God.
>
> (Leviticus 19: 33–34)

People are told that they must treat people from other countries in the same way as they treat their own people. They should think about how it feels to be foreign. They should treat foreigners as equals.

The people are also told that if they employ anyone, they should treat everyone the same. They should not cheat people from other countries, or try not to give them a fair wage:

> **Do not take advantage** of a hired man who is poor and needy, whether he is a brother Israelite or an alien living in one of your towns.
> Pay him his wages each day before sunset, because he is poor and is counting on it. Otherwise he may cry to the LORD against you, and you will be guilty of sin.
>
> (Deuteronomy 24: 14–15)

In the New Testament, there is a famous story called the parable of the Good Samaritan. Christians might use this in a discussion about racism. In the time of Jesus, people did not like Samaritans, because they were mixed race.

> On one occasion an expert in the law stood up to test Jesus. 'Teacher,' he asked, 'what must I do to inherit eternal life?'
>
> 'What is written in the Law?' he replied. 'How do you read it?'
>
> He answered: '"Love the LORD your God with all your heart and with all your soul and with all your strength and with all your mind"; and, "**Love your neighbour as yourself.**"'
>
> 'You have answered correctly,' Jesus replied. 'Do this and you will live.'
>
> But he wanted to justify himself, so he asked Jesus, 'And who is my neighbour?'
>
> In reply Jesus said: 'A man was going down from Jerusalem to Jericho, when he fell into the hands of robbers. They stripped him of his clothes, beat him and went away, leaving him half dead.
>
> A priest happened to be going down the same road, and when he saw the man, he passed by on the other side. So too, a Levite, when he came to the place and saw him, passed by on the other side.
>
> But **a Samaritan**, as he travelled, came where the man was; and when he saw him, he **took pity on him**. He went to him and bandaged his wounds, pouring on oil and wine. Then he put the man on his own donkey, took him to an inn and took care of him.
>
> The next day he took out two silver coins and gave them to the innkeeper. "Look after him," he said, "and when I return, I will reimburse you for any extra expense you may have."
>
> Which of these three do you think was a neighbour to the man who fell into the hands of robbers?'
>
> The expert in the law replied, 'The one who had mercy on him.' Jesus told him, '**Go and do likewise.**'
>
> (Luke 10: 25–37)

PREJUDICE AND EQUALITY

The parable of the Good Samaritan teaches that all people are each other's neighbours

In this parable, Jesus said that people should not just love people from their own race, but should love everyone. Jesus could have made the Samaritan the victim in the story. But the Samaritan was the hero, showing that people from other races should be given respect.

The letters written by the first Christians to the new Churches also say that racism is wrong. In this letter to the Corinthians, the people are told they must change the way they behave now that they are Christians. They should care for all kinds of people.

> But now you must rid yourselves of all such things as these: anger, rage, malice, slander, and filthy language from your lips.
>
> Do not lie to each other, since you have taken off your old self with its practices and have put on the new self, which is being renewed in knowledge in the image of its Creator.
>
> Here **there is no Greek or Jew**, circumcised or uncircumcised, barbarian, Scythian, slave or free, but **Christ is all, and is in all.**
>
> (Colossians 3: 5–11)

CHRISTIAN PERSPECTIVES

The new Church is told that people should not look at what makes them different from each other. They should try to see themselves as one group instead.

Paul's letter to the Galatians gives the same message:

> *You are all sons of God through faith in Christ Jesus, for all of you who were baptised into Christ have clothed yourselves with Christ.*
>
> *There is **neither Jew nor Greek**, slave nor free, male nor female, for **you are all one in Christ Jesus**.*
>
> (Galatians 3: 26–28)

The letter of James teaches that people should not have favourites in the Church. It is wrong to treat some people better than others:

> *My brothers, as believers in our glorious LORD Jesus Christ, **don't show favouritism**.*
>
> *Suppose a man comes into your meeting wearing a gold ring and fine clothes, and a poor man in shabby clothes also comes in. If you show special attention to the man wearing fine clothes and say, 'Here's a good seat for you,' but say to the poor man, 'You stand there' or 'Sit on the floor by my feet,' have you not discriminated among yourselves and become judges with evil thoughts?*
>
> *Listen, my dear brothers: Has not God chosen those who are poor in the eyes of the world to be rich in faith and to inherit the kingdom he promised those who love him?*
>
> *But you have insulted the poor. Is it not the rich who are exploiting you? Are they not the ones who are dragging you into court? Are they not the ones who are slandering the noble name of him to whom you belong?*
>
> *If you really keep the royal law found in Scripture, 'Love your neighbour as yourself,' you are doing right. But if you show favouritism, you sin and are convicted by the law as lawbreakers.*
>
> (James 2: 1–9)

FOR DISCUSSION

Why do you think that Christians have often failed to follow the teaching of the Bible about racism?

IN YOUR NOTES

Make a list of bullet points to show what the Bible teaches about racism. In an exam, you do not have to tell the whole story, you just need to give the main points.

This teaching could be about race and gender (male and female), as well as about rich and poor. It says that people should not judge each other by the way they look. They should show Christian love (agape) to everyone.

THE TEACHING OF THE CHURCHES

Christian Churches today know that they have not always cared equally for people of all races. In the past, some Church leaders were slave traders. Others supported apartheid. But there have been many Christians who thought racism was wrong. In the eighteenth century, the Quakers (members of the Religious Society of Friends) would not have slave traders or slave owners in their Church.

Today, all Churches say there is no place for racism in Christianity. They say it is their belief that God made all people equal, in his image. They say Christians should work against racism. The Church is also trying to make more people of different races welcome in church, and trying to make sure that people from different races are given an equal chance to be Church leaders.

SEXISM

Sexism is another form of prejudice. It is when people believe that one gender is better than the other. Often, people think that men are more important than women.

Many people think that men and women are different in important ways. But some think that because of these differences, women should not have as many choices as men. They think women should work for less pay than men, or they think women should be judged because of how they look, rather than because of the sort of people they are.

Sex discrimination is when women, or sometimes men, are treated unfairly because of their gender. For example, a woman might not get a promotion even if she is better at the job than a man. Or a man might not be given a job as a nurse or a primary school teacher, because people might think he would not do the job as well as a woman.

There are still too few black people as leaders in the Church

CHRISTIAN PERSPECTIVES

There are male nurses, but some people think nursing should just be done by women

In the past, women's lives were different. Before there was contraception that worked, women often spent most of their adult lives having children and looking after them. They often did not get much education.

When factories began, poor women sometimes had jobs there. They were dangerous jobs, and the women were paid less than the men for the same work. Other women who were not as poor had very few jobs to choose from. They were expected to give up working when they got married, to look after their husbands.

Women were not allowed to vote until 1918, after a long struggle. Even then, votes were only for some women, not all of them. It was only in 1928 that women had the same right to vote as men.

During the twentieth century, things began to change for women. The World Wars and changes in the economy meant that it was more accepted for women to have jobs. By the 1960s, 40% of people at work were women. In 1975, the Sex Discrimination Act was passed. This made it against the law for employers to choose between job applicants on the basis of gender. They have to allow both men and women the same

PREJUDICE AND EQUALITY

chances for training and promotion.

Sex discrimination is against the law in the UK, but women still earn less than men and have fewer important posts at work. At least half of all voters are women, but only a small percentage of MPs are women. The majority of people who go to church are women, but some churches do not allow women to be leaders.

Some people think that women should not expect to have the same kind of careers as men. They say that if women want to be mothers, they should not expect their employers to be happy about them needing to have time off when they are pregnant, when the baby is small, or when the children need care. Other people say that women and men should share being parents, and they say employers should try harder to provide working hours that fit in with family life.

THE LEADERSHIP OF CHRISTIAN CHURCHES AND GENDER

Some Churches have always accepted women as leaders and equals with men. These include the **United Reformed Church** and **The Salvation Army**. They say that if someone is the right person to be a leader, it should not matter if they are male or female.

> **FOR DISCUSSION**
>
> Do you think it is reasonable for an employer to prefer to employ men rather than women for some jobs?

Christians disagree strongly about whether women should be priests

CHRISTIAN PERSPECTIVES

Other Churches, such as the **Baptists** and the **Church of England**, have changed their views in the twentieth century. They used to have only men as leaders. The Baptists began having women as ministers in the 1920s. The Church of England began in 1994. Some members of the Church of England were very unhappy about this.

In the **Roman Catholic Church** and the **Eastern Orthodox Church**, women are not allowed to become priests. These Churches say that when the priest celebrates the Eucharist, he is representing Christ. They say it would not be right for a woman to do this. They do not say that men are better than women, but they say that women and men have different talents and skills. These Churches have always given a lot of respect to mothers, for example. The Catechism of the Catholic Church states:

> *Each of the two sexes is an image of the power and tenderness of God, with equal dignity though in a different way.*

The Virgin Mary is seen by many Christians as the ideal woman

Some people think that the views of the Roman Catholic Church about things that affect women are too old-fashioned, such as views about divorce, abortion and contraception. Roman Catholics might say that the way they value women can be seen in the respect shown to the Virgin Mary.

THE BIBLE AND GENDER
(See also Chapter 2 on the roles of husbands and wives, page 18.)

The Bible teaches different things about gender. In many places, it says that men have more rights than women. For example, in the Old Testament, a man is allowed to divorce his wife, but nothing is said about her rights if she wants to divorce him (Deuteronomy 24: 1).

In Old Testament times, society was **patriarchal**. This means that the men were in control. In the Ten Commandments, wives are put in a list as part of a man's property:

IN YOUR NOTES

Write a paragraph explaining why some Christians believe that women should not be priests. Then write another showing why others disagree.

PREJUDICE AND EQUALITY

You shall not covet your neighbour's house. You shall not covet your neighbour's wife, or his manservant or maidservant, his ox or donkey, or anything that belongs to your neighbour.

(Exodus 20: 17)

Deborah, a prophetess, the wife of Lappidoth, was leading Israel at that time. She held court under the Palm of Deborah between Ramah and Bethel in the hill country of Ephraim, and the Israelites came to her to have their disputes decided.

(Judges 4: 4–5)

In the New Testament, sometimes women are told to keep quiet and do what men tell them:

A woman should learn in quietness and full submission. I do not permit a woman to teach, or to have authority over a man; she must be silent.

(1 Timothy 2: 11–12)

In the New Testament, there are women who have important roles. Jesus visited Martha and Mary. He talked to a Samaritan woman at a well. He praised a widow woman for giving all she had to the poor. It was women who were the first to see that Jesus had risen from the dead:

Some people point out that Jesus chose men to be his close followers, not women. They say that this shows that men and not women should be leaders in the Church.

But other parts of the Bible show a different picture. Parts of the New Testament say that women should not speak in church, but in the Old Testament there are women who helped others to follow God. For example, Queen Esther saved the Jews from death. Ruth set an example of love and trust. Huldah was respected and priests asked for her advice. Deborah was a teacher at a time when there were many battles, and people went to her to ask her to sort out their problems:

On the first day of the week, very early in the morning, the women took the spices they had prepared and went to the tomb. They found the stone rolled away from the tomb, but when they entered, they did not find the body of the LORD Jesus. While they were wondering about this, suddenly two men in clothes that gleamed like lightning stood beside them. In their fright the women bowed down with their faces to the ground, but the men said to them, 'Why do you look for the living among the dead? He is not here; he has risen!'

(Luke 24: 1–6)

In Luke's gospel, women were the first to realise that Jesus had risen from the dead

Christians still do not agree about women in the Church. Some people think men and women should be treated the same in every way. Women should be able to be priests and leaders, just like men. They say everyone is made in the image of God, and that God gave his Holy Spirit to men and women equally. Women should not just have to make the tea and arrange the flowers in church.

Other Christians think that men and women have different talents. They think that men and women both matter to God in the same way, but they are different and should do different things.

Some people say that religions such as Christianity have made things worse for women. They say that women have been treated unfairly because of the teachings of the Bible.

CHRISTIAN BELIEFS IN ACTION

Christians believe that all forms of prejudice are wrong, including racism and sexism.

There are many ways that Christians could put their beliefs into action. For example:

- They could try hard not to judge people before they know them well.
- They could make sure people are treated fairly at work.
- They could make it clear to their friends that they do not like racist or sexist jokes.
- They could bring up their children to share their beliefs.
- They could pray about the problems of prejudice.
- They could join a group that works to fight prejudice.
- They could try to make sure that people from ethnic minorities are made to feel welcome in the community.
- They could use their votes to support people who promise to work against prejudice.
- They could take part in a peaceful demonstration against racism or sexism.

PREJUDICE AND EQUALITY

PRACTICE EXAMINATION QUESTIONS

1 (a) Describe the work of one well-known Christian who has worked against racial prejudice. (8 marks)

Remember to choose someone who has made it clear that he or she is a Christian. Martin Luther King or Trevor Huddleston might be good choices. Try to show how their Christian faith has played a part in what they have done.

(b) Explain how Christians might use the teaching of the Bible about prejudice in their daily lives. (7 marks)

This question asks you to show how the teaching of the Bible might be put into practice in ordinary lives. So you need to show that you know what the Bible teaches about prejudice, and give some examples (you might use the parable of the Good Samaritan, for example). You need to give some examples of how Christians might behave – you could use some of the ideas from page 70 in your answer.

(c) 'People are not the same, so there is no reason to treat them as equals.' Do you agree? Give reasons to support your answer, and show that you have thought about different points of view. You must refer to Christianity in your answer. (5 marks)

You might be able to use some of your examples from the Bible here, to support a Christian point of view. Remember to give more than one opinion in your answer, and to support these opinions with reasons.

2 (a) Describe Christian teaching which might be used in a discussion about sexism. (8 marks)

Notice that this question asks about Christian teaching. This means you can use the teaching of the Bible, Church views, and any other Christian ideas. In a discussion about sexism, Christians might not agree with each other.

(b) Explain how and why a Christian might work to make the world a fairer place for people of different races. (7 marks)

To answer this question, you need to think about what Christians believe about racism. You also need to think about what they might do to put these beliefs into action. You could write about the ways an ordinary Christian might behave. You might want to write about the work of a well-known Christian. Try to use several different ideas in your answer.

(c) 'Christians should sometimes use violence to fight against racism.' Do you agree? Give reasons to support your answer, and show that you have thought about different points of view. (5 marks)

Here, you might want to use some of the work from Chapter 5, about violence and non-violent protest, as part of your answer. Perhaps you could use the example of Martin Luther King's non-violent protests. Remember to write about your own point of view.

5

WAR, PEACE AND HUMAN RIGHTS

Christian understandings of a 'Just War'; pacifism, and violent and non-violent protest; human rights, and prisoners of conscience.

The twentieth century was a century of war. There were the First and Second World Wars, which were the biggest the world had ever seen. There were many other wars too, such as the war in Vietnam, the fighting in Northern Ireland, in the Balkans, in the Middle East and in Rwanda. More than 30,000 people are killed every month because of war. Others die too, because their countries are spending so much on the war that they have no money left for things like clean water and hospitals.

Christians believe that war is wrong. They believe that God wants everyone to live in peace. But Christians have different ideas about the best way to get peace. Some say it is never right to use violence. Others say that sometimes, violence has to be used to stop evil.

War destroys lives, homes and communities. This woman's family probably shared many meals in this kitchen; now everything has gone

WAR, PEACE AND HUMAN RIGHTS

BIBLICAL TEACHING ABOUT WAR AND THE USE OF VIOLENCE

The Bible was not written all at the same time. It was written in different times and places. Some parts were written during times when Israel was at peace with other countries, and other parts were written at times of war, or when the people were being ruled by another, stronger nation. There are all sorts of different teachings about war in the Bible. Christians have different views about whether war can be right, and whether people should use violence. The Bible can be used to support different points of view.

CHRISTIAN VIEWS IN SUPPORT OF WAR

In the **Old Testament**, people are sometimes told by God to go to war. They are sometimes told to go and fight so that they can win the Promised Land:

> The LORD your God will drive out those nations before you, little by little. You will not be allowed to eliminate them all at once, or the wild animals will multiply around you. But the LORD **your God will deliver them over to you,** throwing them into great confusion until they are destroyed. He will give their kings into your hand, and you will wipe out their names from under heaven. No one will be able to stand up against you; **you will destroy them.** (Deuteronomy 7: 22–24)

Later, too, the prophets sometimes tell the people that God wants them to go and fight:

> Proclaim this among the nations; **Prepare for war!** Rouse the warriors! Let all the fighting men draw near and attack. Beat your ploughshares into swords and your pruning hooks into spears ...
> (Joel 3: 9–10)

In the **New Testament**, the message is often a message of peace. But in one story, Jesus was angry and violent when he saw that the Temple was being used by cheats:

> On reaching Jerusalem, Jesus entered the temple area and began driving out those who were buying and selling there. He overturned the tables of the money-changers and the benches of those selling doves. (Mark 11: 15)

Some Christians might think this means that it is right to use violence when others are being treated unfairly. Also, they might say that Jesus knew people who were soldiers, but he never told them their job was wrong.

Christians might use these examples in a discussion about war and violence, to support the view that sometimes it is best to fight so that there is justice for everyone.

CHRISTIAN VIEWS OPPOSING VIOLENCE

Not all of the Old Testament is full of war and violence. There is often a message of peace. When the prophet Isaiah spoke about the Messiah who would come, he called him the 'Prince of Peace':

> And he will be called Wonderful Counsellor,
> Mighty God,
> Everlasting Father,
> **Prince of Peace.**
> Of the increase of his government and peace there will be no end. (Isaiah 9: 6–7)

CHRISTIAN PERSPECTIVES

Micah was another prophet. He said that in the future, God would rule over a time of peace. He reminded people of the words of the prophet Joel. He said that one day, weapons would not be needed any more, so they could be made back into farming tools:

> They will beat their swords into ploughshares and their spears into pruning hooks. Nation will not take up sword against nation, nor will they train for war any more. (Micah 4: 3)

Christians might decide that this means they should work to make peace in the world.

There are other examples of teaching about peace in the New Testament:

> Blessed are the peacemakers. (Matthew 5: 9)
>
> Love your enemies, and pray for those who persecute you. (Matthew 5: 44)
>
> If someone strikes you on the right cheek, turn to him the other also. (Matthew 5: 39)
>
> Do not repay evil with evil or insult with insult, but with blessing, because to this you were called so that you may inherit a blessing. (1 Peter 3: 9)

Christians might use these examples to support the view that violence is never right. Jesus taught that people should be loving, even if they are being attacked.

Christians might also say that Jesus did not use violence, even when he was arrested:

> Then the men stepped forward, seized Jesus and arrested him. With that, one of Jesus' companions reached for his sword, drew it out and struck the servant of the High Priest, cutting off his ear.
> 'Put your sword back in its place,' Jesus said to him, 'for all who draw the sword will die by the sword.' (Matthew 26: 52)

They might also point out that the Ten Commandments include the rule:

> You shall not murder. (Exodus 20: 13)

This might mean that killing is never right at all. But others say that the Bible does allow killing in war, and as punishment for serious crimes, so Christians do not all agree about what this rule means.

Christians believe in **agape** (see Chapter 1) which is love for everyone, even enemies. It is difficult for many Christians to see how loving someone could involve killing them in a war.

Teaching about the **sanctity of life** (see Chapter 3) might also mean that killing in a war is wrong, because it means taking away lives that have been made and planned by God.

People who believe that it is never right to use violence are called **pacifists** (see page 78). Some Christians are pacifists.

FOR DISCUSSION

Do you think that killing in a war is the same as murder? If not, what makes it different?

DIFFICULTIES IN INTERPRETING THE BIBLE

Christians have often found it hard to understand why the Bible says different things about war and violence. The Old Testament seems to be full of war and violence, but the New Testament seems to have a message of peace.

Some Christians say that this is because the Old Testament was written before Jesus came. People did not understand so well what God was like, before Jesus showed them.

Other Christians say that the Old

Testament is the word of God, just like the New Testament, so it cannot be wrong about God. They say that the Bible has different views about war because sometimes war is wrong, and sometimes it could be what God wants.

THE ATTITUDES OF CHRISTIAN CHURCHES TO WAR

Christian beliefs about war and violence have changed over the years. In early times, Christians thought it was right to go to war to defend innocent people. They thought it was right to fight a 'holy war', against enemies who were not Christians.

In the Middle Ages, Jerusalem was ruled by Muslims. Christians went to Jerusalem to fight against the Muslims, because they wanted to win Jerusalem back. These wars were called the **Crusades**. The Christians wanted Jerusalem, and they also wanted to stop the Muslims from spreading their empire, and they wanted to keep control of trade routes. At the time, Christian people thought the Crusades were good and right. Some people were fighting because they were greedy, but others thought they had God on their side. When they killed Muslims and Jews, they thought they were fighting against evil.

A lot of people died in the Crusades. The way prisoners were treated was very cruel. The Christians won Jerusalem back, for a time, but then lost it again. Today, Christians look back on the Crusades as something to be ashamed of, because there was so much killing.

In the thirteenth century, St Thomas Aquinas decided people needed rules, so that they could decide if it was right or wrong to go

This painting from the Middle Ages shows one artist's ideas about the Crusade of Peter the Hermit

to war. He used other people's ideas, too. The rules he made are called the **Just War** theory. Aquinas said a war was only 'just' (meaning 'fair', or 'right') if it matched the following:

1. A war should be started by people in charge, like a government or king, not just anybody.
2. There must be a good reason for starting a war. Greed is not a good reason.
3. The reason for going to war must be to do good.
4. War must only be used if everything else has been tried first.
5. The war must do more good than harm.
6. It must be possible to win. There is no point in going to war if the enemy is clearly much more powerful, because people will be killed for nothing.
7. The war must be fought fairly, and people must not be any more cruel than they have to be.

CHRISTIAN PERSPECTIVES

Before the First World War, most Churches supported their countries when they were at war. But the First World War was worse than anything they had ever seen before. Nine million people died. Twenty-one million more were badly hurt. Some Christians began to think that maybe it had been wrong to support the war.

When the Second World War began in 1939, most of the Christian Churches agreed that it was important to fight against Hitler. But there were also many people who were not happy about the way the war was fought. They thought that it did not fit in with the rules about the Just War, because too many innocent people were killed.

At the end of the Second World War, the first atomic bombs were dropped on the Japanese cities of Hiroshima and Nagasaki. Thousands of people died instantly. The radiation from the bomb killed many others. After the bombs, many babies were born dead or born disabled, and children suffered from cancer. Some Christians thought that it was right to drop the bombs, because it made the war with Japan end quickly. But others said it was very wrong, and was against all Christian teaching. They said it should never be allowed to happen again.

Wars changed a lot in the twentieth century. In the First World War, nearly all the people who were killed were soldiers. In wars today, 95% of the people killed are civilians (people who are not soldiers), including old people, women and children. The Churches have to think about several different issues:

After the First World War, some Christians began to think they had been wrong to support the fighting

WAR, PEACE AND HUMAN RIGHTS

- Whether the Church should encourage Christians to fight for their country in war time;
- Whether the Church should support the country if it wants to build its stores of nuclear weapons;
- Whether the Church should support people who refuse to go to war for religious reasons (**conscientious objectors**, see page 78).

The **Church of England** teaches that sometimes wars have to happen, to stop something even worse from happening. It says that people have the right to make up their own minds about whether they should fight in a war. The Church of England also says that the UK needs some nuclear weapons, to stop other countries from attacking it, but it says that all countries should work together to get rid of nuclear weapons.

The **Roman Catholic Church** agrees, and says that nuclear weapons should only be used to prevent wars, and should never be used to attack. The Churches say that all Christians should pray for peace.

Christians have made a new set of Just War rules, to fit in with modern kinds of war. The rules say:

1. Going to war must be a response to an unjust attack. Christians should never be the first to attack.
2. There must be a real chance of winning.
3. After a war, the country that loses should be treated fairly.
4. Christians should only attack military targets, not ordinary people.
5. When force is used, it should be for a good reason.

Hiroshima – modern nuclear weapons can destroy huge areas. Christians disagree about whether the country needs to have them

CHRISTIAN PERSPECTIVES

Since the Second World War, Churches have taken part in discussions about chemical weapons. They have joined with others to try and ban the use of landmines.

SUMMARY

Many Christian Churches think that war can sometimes be the only answer to sort out a problem between countries. They say that Christians should defend the weak, and it would be wrong to do nothing if people are suffering.

PACIFISM

The **Religious Society of Friends** (Quakers) takes a different view. Quakers believe that war is never right. They know that there is evil in the world, but they say that fighting is not the right way to get rid of evil. They say that Christians should use 'weapons of the Spirit' – love, truth and peace. Quakers think it is wrong to have or use nuclear weapons.

People who think it is always wrong to use violence are called **pacifists**.

Quakers and other pacifists say that people should work to get rid of evil, but they should do it in a non-violent, peaceful way.

In a war, people who are strongly against fighting are called **conscientious objectors**. Their consciences tell them to object to war. In war time, they refuse to fight as soldiers, or to make weapons. Instead, they work as nurses, or carry stretchers, or drive ambulances.

Not all pacifists are Christians. But some Christians might choose to be pacifists, because of the teaching in the Bible about peace (see pages 73–74). In the 1980s, there was a new interest in a movement called the Campaign for Nuclear Disarmament (CND). This worked to get rid of nuclear weapons. One of its leaders was Bruce Kent, a Roman Catholic priest.

IN YOUR NOTES

(a) Explain why some Christians think that it can be right to go to war. Use examples from the Bible in your answer.
(b) Explain what 'pacifists' are.
(c) Explain why some Christians are pacifists.

NON-VIOLENT PROTEST

Some people think that it is always best to use non-violent protest in times of conflict. They believe that whatever happens, violence is not the right answer. Non-violent protest is not the same as doing nothing. It can take many different forms, such as marches, demonstrations, boycotts, sit-ins and the use of the vote. But sometimes it is dangerous for people to use these methods. In some countries, people are not allowed to protest and, if they try, they are attacked by the police.

Martin Luther King (see page 60), for example, believed it was wrong to use violence against racism. He was treated violently, but he used peaceful protests. He believed that using violence makes the victim as bad as the person who is attacking.

WAR, PEACE AND HUMAN RIGHTS

HUMAN RIGHTS

The Universal Declaration of Human Rights was written after the Second World War. People had seen how badly human beings can treat each other, and they wanted to agree on some basic human rights.

There are 30 articles of human rights in the declaration. These are some of them:

Article 1: 'All human beings are born free and equal in dignity and rights.'
This means that all people are born with the same human rights as everyone else in the world. All people should be treated with respect.

Article 2: 'Everyone is entitled to all the rights and freedoms set forth in this Declaration, without distinction of any kind.'
This means that your rights are the same, no matter what sort of person you are. It should not matter where people come from, or what their beliefs are, or whether they are male or female, or

Non-violent protest is not always easy. This Chinese student chose to protest against his government in Tiananmen Square

FOR DISCUSSION

Do you think non-violent protest can work? Why do some people choose non-violent protest, instead of hitting back?

what colour they are, or how much money or power they have.

Article 3: 'Everyone has the right to life, liberty and security of person.'
We all have the right to live in freedom and safety. No one should be killed, or kept in prison without good reasons.

Article 5: 'No one shall be subjected to torture or to cruel, inhuman or degrading treatment or punishment.'
This means that torture is always wrong. If people have to be punished, it should be in a way that still respects them. This applies in police stations and prisons, in time of peace and in time of war.

Article 9: 'No one shall be subject to arbitrary arrest, detention or exile.'
People may not be arrested or held in a police station or prison without a good reason. They may not be kept out of their own country for no good reason.

Article 18: 'Everyone has the right to freedom of thought, conscience and religion.'
People have the right to their own beliefs. No one should be able to treat them badly just because of their opinions or religion.

These articles, and many others, have been agreed by all the countries in the United Nations. The Christian Churches all support the Universal Declaration of Human Rights. People can go to an international court if they think that their rights have not been respected.

Although these rules were written, there are still many countries where people do not have basic human rights. People who disagree with the government just 'disappear'. They are taken away by the police and put in prison or killed, and their families never find out what happened to them. Sometimes, people who say the government is wrong are tortured or killed. People with power and money commit crimes, and no one does anything about it. Poor people do not get fair trials in court.

Some people are 'prisoners of conscience'. They are locked up just because of their religion or politics. Sometimes, they are locked up just because of their colour or language.

Christians believe that all people have human rights, because they were all made by God. They believe God loves each person. Christians try to show the love of God by standing up for the poor and weak. Some Christians are in favour of Liberation Theology. Some Christians support groups such as Amnesty International, which works for human rights.

LIBERATION THEOLOGY

Many people are lucky enough to live in countries where they can say what they think. They can tell the government if they disagree with it. For example, in the UK, people can use their votes to show the government what they think. They can go on marches. They can write or talk to their MPs. If they think the police have been unfair to them, they can complain. But in some countries, this does not happen. People who disagree with the government are put in prison, or killed, often without a fair trial. If people are treated unfairly, they have to keep quiet or they are in danger.

Liberation theology is a way of thinking that some Christians support. It says that Christians should join together with poor people and people who are not treated fairly. Christians should help these people to speak out if they are not given their basic human rights. People who agree with liberation theology say it is not enough just to be kind to the poor. They have to act, so that the government changes and the people are not poor and weak any more.

Liberation theology has been important in Latin America. In countries such as El Salvador and Chile, a few rich people have most of the money, and other people are very poor. These are Roman Catholic countries. Some Roman Catholic priests have taken up liberation theology, and have put their lives at risk to try and help the poor to get fair treatment. Some have been put in prison, tortured, and even killed because of their beliefs.

Some followers of liberation theology think that human rights are so important that it can be right to use violence, to defend the weak.

Camilo Torres was a Roman Catholic priest who used violence to help the poor. He lived in Colombia. The government was unfair, and many people did not have proper food or clothes. People who argued with the government were taken away in secret. Men, women and children were sometimes killed, without having a fair trial. Everyone was afraid of the government.

Camilo Torres believed that Christians should stand up and do something to help, when people are being treated badly. He joined a group of freedom fighters. He called on all Christians to join in the fight for human rights for the poor.

Camilo Torres said that revolution was something that Christians should all be involved in. He was killed in action, in 1966.

Oscar Romero was a Roman Catholic archbishop. He lived in El Salvador. He spoke in church about the need to defend the poor and weak. He did not agree with the government of El Salvador, and spoke about this in public. In 1980, while he was celebrating Mass, armed men came into the church and shot him dead in front of the altar. They also killed other people who had listened to him.

There are still many Christians who believe that liberation theology is right, even though it can be dangerous for them.

Oscar Romero, a Catholic priest, who was shot dead while celebrating mass, because of his support for the poor of El Salvador

CHRISTIAN PERSPECTIVES

> **FOR DISCUSSION**
>
> Why do some Christians think that violence might be needed to make the world a fairer place? Why do other Christians disagree?

AMNESTY INTERNATIONAL

Amnesty International is an organisation that works to help people who are not being allowed their human rights. It began in 1961. It was started by a British lawyer called Peter Benenson. He read a story in a newspaper about two students who had been sent to prison for seven years, just because they had raised their glasses in a toast to freedom, in a bar in Lisbon, Portugal. He thought that governments should not be able to get away with treating people in this sort of way, and he decided to get together with other people who felt the same way, to do something about it.

The aims of Amnesty International are:

- to free prisoners of conscience (people who are in prison because of their beliefs)
- to get fair trials for political prisoners
- to end torture, killings and people 'disappearing'
- to get rid of the death penalty in every country.

Amnesty International finds out about cases where it seems someone is not being given his or her human rights. The organisation makes sure it has as many facts as possible. Then the members start writing letters to tell as many people as they can about what is going on. Countries that use torture or killing, or that put people in prison without fair trials, often do this in secret. If everyone is told what they are doing, they might be made to stop.

For example, if someone is kept in prison without a fair trial and is tortured, and no one knows, it will carry on. But if a group such as Amnesty International finds out about the prisoner, and lots of its members write to the government of the country about the prisoner, and they send the prisoner hundreds of letters and cards of support, then the government might think again. It will see that people know what is going on. It might stop the torture, and let the prisoner go.

I was being kept naked in an underground cell. When the first 200 letters came, the guards gave me back my clothes. The next 200 letters came and the prison officers came to see me. When the next pile of letters arrived, the director got in touch with his superior. The letters kept coming, 3,000 of them, and the President called me to

Amnesty International is not a Christian organisation, but Christians might choose to support it

WAR, PEACE AND HUMAN RIGHTS

his office. He showed me an enormous box of letters he had received, and said: How is it that a trade union leader like you has so many friends all over the world?

(Union leader in the Dominican Republic, campaigned for by Amnesty International)

Amnesty International says it is very important to know the facts before starting letter-writing. It has a research department, which finds out as much as possible about the people in prison and why they are there. It also sends people to watch trials and to meet the prisoners and people in the government. When it knows the facts, the members get organised to start their letter-writing.

Amnesty International tries to give as much help as it can. It tries to get the prisoners seen by doctors. Sometimes, it raises money for food and clothes, and gives the prisoners help after they have been set free.

Amnesty International works to try and change the laws, to protect people's human rights. It worked to change the laws about using torture. It worked to ban the death penalty in the UK, and in other countries. It also helped to set up an international court of justice, so that people can be put on trial for doing wrong without their governments protecting them.

Amnesty International is against the death penalty (capital punishment) in all cases. Its research department says that the death penalty has never made

Amnesty International helps people when their human rights have been taken away

TORTURE

STAMP OUT TORTURE

DON'T LET THEM GET AWAY WITH IT

JOIN **AMNESTY INTERNATIONAL'S**
CAMPAIGN TO STAMP OUT TORTURE

Amnesty International,
99-119 Rosebery Avenue,
London, EC1R 4RE
http://www.amnesty.org.uk
CAMPAIGN HOTLINE: 020 7417 6385

CHRISTIAN PERSPECTIVES

ICT FOR RESEARCH

Visit the web-site of Amnesty International:

www.amnesty.org.uk

Find out more about the campaigns, and the ways in which Amnesty International is supported by its local branches.

crime rates go down. Its members say that the death penalty goes against human rights, and is the worst form of torture. When people are given a death sentence, Amnesty International tries to get the sentence changed.

Amnesty International has been given awards for its work with human rights. In 1977, it was given the Nobel Peace Prize, and in 1978, it was given the United Nations Human Rights Prize.

CHRISTIANS AND AMNESTY INTERNATIONAL

Amnesty International is not a Christian organisation. But many Christians support it, because it is a way of putting Christian beliefs into practice. Joining together with others gives people more power to do something about human rights. Christians might feel that joining Amnesty International is a good way of showing their beliefs that every life matters to God. It could be a good way of putting agape (Christian love) into practice.

WAR, PEACE AND HUMAN RIGHTS

PRACTICE EXAMINATION QUESTIONS

1 (a) Describe Biblical teaching that might be used to support pacifism. (8 marks)

In this question you are asked to use teaching from the Bible. Remember that pacifism means believing that violence is always wrong. You need to include some teaching from the Bible about peace, and explain what it means.

(b) Explain why some Christians might choose to fight for their countries in times of war. (7 marks)

You could explain Christian teaching about the need to defend the weak. You might want to include ideas such as the Just War theory. Try to think of more than one reason why a Christian might choose to fight, and remember to write about Christian reasons rather than just general reasons.

(c) 'The Bible was written too long ago to have anything useful to say about wars today.' Do you agree? Give reasons to support your answer, and show that you have thought about different points of view. You must refer to Christianity in your answer. (5 marks)

In this answer, you need to give different opinions and support them with reasons. Why might some people think that the Bible does not say anything useful for today, about war? (Think about how war has changed, for example.) Why might some people think it is still useful? What might a Christian think? You might think of using some of the information from Chapter 1 (Background) to say why the Bible is important for Christians.

2 (a) Describe Christian teaching about human rights. (8 marks)

Remember to show that you know the Universal Declaration of Human Rights is not Christian, although Christians support it. Try to give Christian teachings about why human lives are important, such as teaching about the sanctity of life, loving your neighbour, looking after the poor and so on.

(b) Explain why Christians might choose to support the work of an organisation that helps the victims of human rights abuses. (7 marks)

Remember that Amnesty International is not a Christian organisation, but Christians might support it. You need to show how this fits in with Christian beliefs, so you need to say something about why Christians think human life is important and why Christians should take care of other people.

(c) 'Sometimes, using violence is the best way to fight against injustice.' Do you agree? Give reasons to support your answer, and show that you have thought about different points of view. You must refer to Christianity in your answer. (5 marks)

Remember to give more than one point of view, including a Christian opinion. Say why some people believe violence is always wrong – you might be able to think of some examples of people who have used non-violent protest. Say why other people might think that violence might be needed – perhaps you could mention Camilo Torres or Oscar Romero.

CHRISTIAN RESPONSIBILITY FOR THE PLANET

Christian teaching relating to the problems facing the planet: the world as the creation of God, the concept of stewardship, environmental issues and Christian responses to them.

BIBLICAL TEACHING – THE WORLD AS THE CREATION OF GOD

When you open a book, the first sentence often tells you something about the sort of book you are about to read. It sets the scene. The Bible is just like this. The first words of the Bible are some of the most famous:

> *In the beginning God created the heavens and the earth.*
>
> (Genesis 1: 1)

The Bible teaches that the planet was created by God, and belongs to God

CHRISTIAN RESPONSIBILITY FOR THE PLANET

It says that God was there at the very beginning of the world. The world was made by God.

In the creation story, God makes everything that, goes in the earth and the skies. Each time something is made, the Bible says: 'And God saw that it was good'. The Bible seems to say that, at the start, there was nothing wrong with the planet. It all worked very well.

The Bible always says that the world belongs to God. Many of the Psalms praise God for making the world:

> For the LORD is the great God, the great King above all gods. In his hand are the depths of the earth, and the mountain peaks belong to him. The sea is his, for he made it, and his hands formed the dry land. Come, let us bow down in worship, let us kneel before the LORD our Maker.
> (Psalm 95: 3–6)

> The earth is the LORD's, and everything in it, the world, and all who live in it; for he founded it upon the seas and established it upon the waters.
> (Psalm 24: 1–2)

Psalm 19 says that the skies show the glory of God:

> The heavens declare the glory of God; the skies proclaim the work of his hands. Day after day they pour forth speech; night after night they display knowledge. There is no speech or language where their voice is not heard. Their voice goes out into all the earth, their words to the ends of the world.
> (Psalm 19: 1–4)

The Psalm goes on to talk about the laws of God in the world. It says that God made the laws of science, and God made rules about how people should behave. This Psalm teaches that God is in control of the whole universe. People should keep to God's laws. They are as perfect as the ways the planets move.

The New Testament does not say as much about God making the world. But there are parts that say that God made everything and cares for all living things:

> Look at the birds of the air; they do not sow or reap or store away in barns, and yet your heavenly Father feeds them. Are you not much more valuable than they? ... See how the lilies of the field grow. They do not labour or spin. Yet I tell you that not even Solomon in all his splendour was dressed like one of these.
> (Matthew 6: 26–29)

THE CONCEPT OF STEWARDSHIP

The first law that humans were given when they were made was that they should be 'stewards' of the earth. A steward is someone who acts as a caretaker. For example, a steward at a music festival might show people where to park their cars, or help lost children find their parents, and deal with First Aid and help people to be safe. A 'shop steward' is a member of a Trade Union, who looks after the workers and makes sure they are treated fairly. So being a steward means working for the owner or organiser. It means serving others, looking after the weakest, making sure that everything is as it should be, and keeping things safe.

When humans are made as stewards of the earth, they are given this same caretaking role:

CHRISTIAN PERSPECTIVES

Christians believe that the beauty of the world shows something of what God is like

*Then God said, 'Let us make man in our image, in our likeness, and let them rule over the fish of the sea and the birds of the air, over the livestock, over all the earth, and over all the creatures that move along the ground.' So God created man in his own image, **in the image of God** he created him; male and female he created them. God blessed them and said to them, 'Be fruitful and increase in number; fill the earth and subdue it. **Rule over the fish of the sea and the birds of the air and over every living creature that moves on the ground.'***

Then God said, 'I give you every seed-bearing plant on the face of the whole earth and every tree that has fruit with seed in it. They will be yours for food. And to all the beasts of the earth and the birds of the air and all the creatures that move on the ground – everything that has the breath of life in it – I give every green plant for food.' And it was so. God saw all that he had made, and it was very good.

(Genesis 1: 26–31)

People are in charge of all the living things that have been made on the earth. But they do not own them. They have to look after the world, which belongs to God.

In another Psalm, the writer looks at the night sky and thinks about the beauty of the world. He thinks about what a big task it is, to be a steward of the world:

O LORD, our Lord, how majestic is your name in all the earth!

You have set your glory above the heavens …

When I consider your heavens, the work of your fingers, the moon and the stars, which you have set in place, what is man that you are mindful of him, the son of man that you care for him?

You made him a little lower than the heavenly beings and crowned him with glory and honour.

You made him ruler over the works of your hands; you put everything under his feet.

(Psalm 8: 1, 3–6)

CHRISTIAN RESPONSIBILITY FOR THE PLANET

Some of the rules of the Old Testament are about being a good steward. For example, rules are given about the harvest. In Old Testament times, people used to do something called 'gleaning'. After a field had been harvested, any grain left on the ground was left for the poor. They could go and collect it and use it. The book of Ruth has a scene where Ruth went to Bethlehem after the barley harvest, to glean. She met her second husband Boaz here. Boaz is seen as a good man, because he allowed poor people to glean on his land.

'Gleaning' was a way in which poor people could find food, by gathering the grain the harvesters had left behind. Painting by J. F. Millet

> When you are harvesting in your field and you overlook a sheaf, do not go back and get it. Leave it for the alien, the fatherless and the widow, so that the LORD your God may bless you in all the work of your hands. When you beat the olives from your trees, do not go over the branches a second time. Leave what remains for the alien, the fatherless and the widow. When you harvest the grapes in your vineyard, do not go over the vines again. **Leave what remains for the alien, the fatherless and the widow.** Remember that you were slaves in Egypt. That is why I command you to do this.
>
> (Deuteronomy 24: 19–22)

The law tells people not to take every last scrap for themselves. They should leave something for the people who will come after them.

CHRISTIAN PERSPECTIVES

PROBLEMS FACING THE PLANET

All our water, food, medicines and fuel come from the world's natural resources. But the number of people on the planet has grown very quickly. We are using up these resources, and many of them cannot be replaced.

THE OZONE LAYER

The ozone layer is a layer of oxygen all around the earth. It protects the earth from ultra-violet rays from the sun. But some of the ozone layer has been destroyed, because humans have used CFC gases in aerosols and refrigerators. There are large holes in the ozone layer. The ultra-violet rays can get through, and cause eye problems and skin cancers. Children in Australia are often not allowed to play out in the sun unless they wear big hats. Some children in Australia have started getting skin cancer even when they are at primary school, because of the hole in the ozone layer.

In Australia, children wear large shady hats and keep covered up, to protect them from skin cancers

CHRISTIAN RESPONSIBILITY FOR THE PLANET

When rainforests are destroyed, it puts wildlife at risk

GLOBAL WARMING

One of the biggest problems facing the planet is climate change. This is often called 'global warming'. There is a thin layer of gases around the earth, which provide the right climate for all different life forms. But if there is too much of one kind of gas and not enough of other gases, then the climate changes. The earth is slowly becoming warmer.

Too much carbon dioxide is being produced in the world. Some of it is because rainforests are being cut down. Some is because of cars, and some is produced by factories. Burning fuels, such as coal and oil, also makes carbon dioxide.

Scientists warn that global warming could soon be very dangerous. If the earth gets much warmer, ice caps at the North and South Poles will melt, and the sea levels will rise. This will cause storms, hurricanes and floods.

DEFORESTATION

Half of the world's rainforests have been destroyed since the Second World War. 'Deforestation' means clearing away forests. The wood is sold by timber companies. The land is used for something else, such as farming, mining or building. The rainforests only cover about 6% of the world, but they contain more than 50% of all species of animals and plants.

Every week, an area of rainforest the size of the UK is cleared. Many animals and plants have become extinct, because the area where they lived has been destroyed. We do not yet know what the effects of deforestation will be on the earth.

CHRISTIAN PERSPECTIVES

Rubbish from houses and factories causes pollution

POLLUTION

Pollution affects the world in many different ways. Many countries produce a lot of waste. They produce poisonous gases, which cause breathing problems and acid rain. They produce nuclear waste, which poisons the sea, and causes cancer and birth defects. They also produce other forms of waste, which are difficult to get rid of in safe ways. An average of a tonne of rubbish is produced for each house in the UK every year, and another tonne of toxic waste per person in produced by industry. Farmers also use chemicals to help the crops to grow, and these can harm rivers and wildlife, and affect drinking water.

ENVIRONMENTAL DAMAGE TO THE SEAS

Damage to the seas is important because so much of the earth's surface is covered by sea. It is a very difficult problem to control, because the sea does not belong to any one country and no one is responsible for protecting it. People dump waste in the sea, such as toxic waste, nuclear waste and raw sewage. The seas have been over-fished, so there are fewer fish in the sea than ever before. Fish are a very important food for many of the world's poorest countries.

THE INVOLVEMENT OF THE CHRISTIAN CHURCHES

Some people think that the Christian Churches should take some of the blame for problems with the environment. They say Christianity has taught that people can rule over other animals and plants. It makes people think they can do what they like, and can kill other animals for food, for fur or even for fun. It makes people think they are more important than anything else on the planet.

Christianity teaches that humans are set apart from other animals, because they are made in the image of God. Other people might say that humans are the most intelligent species, but this does not give them the right to kill or make other

CHRISTIAN RESPONSIBILITY FOR THE PLANET

animals suffer.

Today, the Churches are much more aware of problems of the environment. They know that people have failed to be good stewards.

The Churches have had many discussion groups to try and find ways for Christians to help the environment.

The **Church of England** has agreed to try and reduce pollution, to use energy carefully, to look after animals and plants, and to help control human population.

The **Roman Catholic Church** teaches that people should try to waste less. It says we should think about the people of the future, and also think about the way rich countries affect the lives of the poor.

All the Churches agree that looking after the planet, as a good steward, is an important part of being a Christian. They say that agape (Christian love) is for people who will live in the future, as well as people today.

ICT FOR RESEARCH

Visit the Church of England web-site on:

www.cofe.anglican.org/

Go to the section called 'The Church of England's view on …' and read the statements that have been made on the environment and animal welfare.

CHRISTIAN RESPONSES TO ENVIRONMENTAL ISSUES

Christians might put their faith into action in different ways:

- They could use their votes to support people who care about the environment.
- They could pray about the problems of the environment.
- They could cut down on waste at home. They could recycle, for example by using bottle banks.
- They could try to use less fuel in the home.
- They could share lifts, or walk or cycle to work, to cut down on car pollution and fuel waste.
- They could join protest marches about the environment.
- They could join an organisation that works to help the environment.

FOR DISCUSSION

Why do you think that many people do not care much about the environment?

ICT FOR RESEARCH

Visit the Christian ecology web-site:

www.christian-ecology.org.uk/

Find out more about how care for the environment relates to Christian beliefs.

93

CHRISTIAN PERSPECTIVES

ORGANISATIONS WHICH CHRISTIANS MIGHT CHOOSE TO SUPPORT

There are many groups that try to help the environment. Three of the most famous are Greenpeace, the Worldwide Fund for Nature and Friends of the Earth. All of them try to get the government to change its rules and reduce waste and damage. For example, Greenpeace has worked on a new way of cooling, to produce refrigerators that do not damage the environment. It is trying to get countries all around the world to use 'Greenfreeze' ways of cooling.

Friends of the Earth is a leading group in the UK. It has many small local groups. It uses funds to research new ways of helping the environment. It tries to get the government to use energy sources, such as wind turbines, sea power and solar power, which do not waste fuel.

The Worldwide Fund for Nature has a Living Planet campaign. It tries to make people aware of the number of animals and plants that are becoming extinct. It has four main areas of campaign: Climate Change, Endangered Seas, Forests for Life and Living Waters.

None of these organisations is run by Christians. But Christians might choose to support them, because they might think that these groups agree with important Christian beliefs, such as stewardship and care for other people, including the people of the future.

Scientists are working to develop new ways of creating energy without wasting natural resources

ICT FOR RESEARCH

Visit one or more of the following web-sites to find out more about the work of organisations which aim to conserve the environment.
Friends of the Earth:
www.foe.co.uk/
Greenpeace:
www.greenpeace.org/

IN YOUR NOTES

Write about the work of the organisation you have chosen. Give some examples of the projects it is working on at the moment.

CHRISTIAN RESPONSIBILITY FOR THE PLANET

PRACTICE EXAMINATION QUESTION

1 (a) Describe Christian teaching about stewardship. (8 marks)

Remember to use examples from the Bible in your answer, as well as teaching from the Churches. You do not have to learn long passages of the Bible off by heart. It is a good idea to know some short phrases, such as 'the image of God', or 'the earth is the Lord's', and explain what they mean to a Christian. You might want to use page 93 and say what the Churches teach about the environment.

(b) Explain how a Christian might show concern for the world's environmental problems. (7 marks)

Here you are asked to show what a Christian might do, to show care for the environment. There are lots of examples on page 93 that you might use. Try to give some different ideas and examples, rather than spending your whole answer writing about just one idea.

(c) 'The environment is a problem for governments. People on their own cannot do anything about it.' Do you agree? Give reasons to support your answer, and show that you have thought about different points of view. You must refer to Christianity in your answer. (5 marks)

Do you think that problems of the environment need to be tackled only by governments? Or do you think that all people could do something, even if it is only small? What do you think a Christian would say about this? Try to include different points of view in your answer, and make sure that you include what a Christian would say.

CHRISTIAN RESPONSIBILITY TOWARDS DISADVANTAGED PEOPLE

> **Christian attitudes towards the poor and the weak. Biblical teaching, the responses of the Churches to poverty, and the work of at least one explicitly Christian aid organisation, e.g. Christian Aid, CAFOD or Tearfund.**

WORLD POVERTY: THE NORTH-SOUTH DIVIDE

Some countries in the world are very rich and others are very poor. Most of the rich countries are north of the Equator: the USA, Western European countries, including the UK, and Japan, for example. These are often called the Developed World. Only a quarter of the world's population lives in the Developed World. But these countries use up more than three quarters of the world's resources (food, fuel etc) every year. There is enough food in the world for everyone to have enough. But because people in the rich North want to have so much, the people in the South have to go without.

Australia and New Zealand are also rich countries, but most of the other countries south of the Equator are very poor, including South America, Africa and India. These are known as the Developing World or the Third World.

This difference between North and South is called the **North-South divide**.

In the Developed World, most people expect to live until they are 70 or more, and to be educated until they are at least 16. People choose how many children to have, and expect them all to survive. Children of ten get lots of pocket money. People in the Developed World have problems with heart disease and obesity (being overweight), but they also have good health care. They own most of the world's factories, and they control world banks.

But in the Developing World, many people die before they are 50. More than half the people in some countries are aged under 14. This means that the country needs more food than it can produce. One child in seven dies before reaching the age of five. Most of the people in the Developing World have an income of less than £1.25 a week. People are hungry and do not have the right kinds of food. Few people have safe clean water. There are not enough doctors, and not enough people can read. The poor countries have to borrow money from the rich countries, and when they pay it back, they are poorer than ever, because of high interest rates.

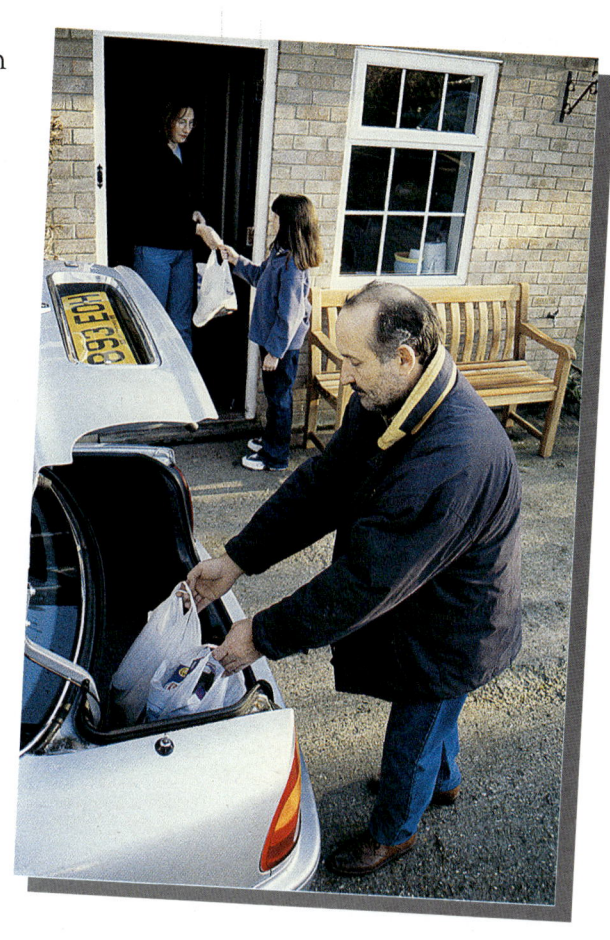

SOME STATISTICS

For every 1000 people in Canada, there are 221 doctors. For every 1000 people in Haiti, there are 16.

A woman in the UK lives for about 79.4 years. In Bangladesh, she can expect to reach 57.

The Developed World owns 94% of the world's health care. So 6% is left for the other three quarters of the world's people.

(Statistics supplied by CAFOD, 2000)

Mali, in western Africa, uses only eight litres of water for each person each day. This water has to be used for everything – drinking, cooking, washing and laundry. In the UK, this amount of water is used every time someone flushes a toilet.

The money that people in Europe spend on ice cream each year would be enough to pay for clean water for everyone in developing countries.

(Statistics supplied by Tearfund, 2000)

In rich countries, people can buy whatever they need. They do not have to worry about food, houses or clean water

World poverty is a very big problem. There are many reasons why so many people are so poor. The biggest reason is that rich people do not want to change the way they live. Even when rich countries give to the poor, they often make the poor pay it back with extra added on.

THE BRANDT REPORT

In 1980, a document called the Brandt Report was written. It was the result of research into what makes people poor, and what should be done about it. It was decided that the best thing to do would be to change things for everyone, not just the poor, to share things more fairly. This should be done over a long time, not just when there is a crisis.

But although the Brandt Report explained many things, nothing much has changed for the poor.

CHRISTIAN PERSPECTIVES

Things will only change for people in the Developing World if rich countries change the way they live

THE CAUSES OF POVERTY

POPULATION

Many people believe that one of the main reasons why poorer countries stay poor is that they have too many children. Some people say they should have smaller families. But it is not as easy as this. People in poor countries need to have large families in order to survive. They cannot grow their crops without help, but they are too poor to employ other adults, so they have children who can work for them. There is no state care for the elderly, so children are needed so that they can look after their parents when they are too old to look after themselves. Many babies die, so families need to have enough to live to be adults. In rich countries, people do not need to have many children, and so their families are smaller; but they still eat most of the world's food.

CHRISTIAN RESPONSIBILITY TOWARDS DISADVANTAGED PEOPLE

DISASTERS

Disasters seem to happen often in the Developing World. We see stories nearly every day in the newspapers and on television of famines and floods. Sometimes, we might not even be interested, because we see it so often. But disasters like famines and floods have terrible effects on poor countries. Because the people are poor, they cannot afford safe places to live – those are already taken by people who have more money. Because they are poor, they have homes which fall down easily. Because the country is poor, it does not have a supply of extra food and medicines when disasters happen. Rich countries can prepare emergency supplies, but poor countries have no money for extra supplies.

A flood in Bangladesh leaves many people with nothing

CHRISTIAN PERSPECTIVES

CONFLICT

One of the causes of poverty is war. When countries go to war, they have to spend money on weapons, when the money could have been used for schools, doctors or farms. Landmines make areas unsuitable to farm. War needs soldiers, when the people could have been planting crops. Transport is much more difficult, so food supplies do not reach the people who need them. People lose their homes, or they leave an area because it is too dangerous, and they become refugees.

DEBT AND FAIR TRADE

In many developing countries debt is a major problem. The countries have to borrow money to survive. The debts have to be paid with interest, and the countries often end up owing far more than they can afford to pay back. They have to cut down on areas such as health care and education, so that they can pay back the money.

The rich in the North buy goods, such as sugar, cotton and coffee, from the poor South. The South uses the money to help build economies and to pay off money that was borrowed. But the poor countries receive lower and lower prices for their goods. The rich people in the North want to be able to shop cheaply. The major supermarket chains have 'price wars' to see which can get the most customers. The buyers in the North only offer the growers in the South very little money.

The poor have to grow more to sell, to try and keep up. They have to sell everything, and cannot keep enough for themselves. They have to borrow more money, and they get poorer.

A project called **Jubilee 2000** was set up to try and put pressure on governments to cancel world debt. People wanted the poorest countries to be able to use their money to supply basic needs, rather than having to spend it on repayments. The Church called the year 2000 a Jubilee year, because it remembered two thousand years of Christianity. In the Bible, a rule is made that in the Year of Jubilee, debts are to be cancelled and slaves are to be freed:

> *He and his children are to be released in the Year of Jubilee.*
> (Leviticus 25: 54)

IN YOUR NOTES

(a) Why does the Developing World owe money to rich countries?
(b) What happens to poor people when their countries owe money?
(c) Make a list of the main causes of poverty in the Developing World.

CHRISTIAN RESPONSIBILITY TOWARDS DISADVANTAGED PEOPLE

Many different Christians from around the world joined together to protest against world debt and to campaign for change.

People in the Developing World often have to work in ways that are against the law in the UK. They have to work for long hours, and they get paid very little. Sometimes they earn only 40p each day. They cannot buy the things they need, or send their children to school. Often, big companies control everything in the town, such as the shops, schools and hospitals, so the workers cannot complain or else they lose everything.

The Fairtrade Mark is used by some companies to show that their products have been made by workers who are treated fairly. To get the Fairtrade Mark on their products, companies have to pay a fair wage and make sure the workers are safe. Fairtrade tea, coffee, chocolate and honey can be found in shops such as Oxfam.

People who want to put the Fairtrade Mark on their products have to do these things:

- They have to pay the workers a fair wage.
- They have to be fair about the way they give out jobs, and look after the poorest people.
- They have to make sure that they produce their goods in a way that does not harm the environment.
- They have to show care for the health and safety of the workers.

'Then they also will answer, "Lord, when was it that we saw you hungry or thirsty or a stranger or naked or sick or in prison, and did not take care of you?"' (Matthew 25: 44)

FOR DISCUSSION

Do you think that the Developed World could do something about world debt? If so, what could it do?

CHRISTIAN PERSPECTIVES

The Fairtrade Mark means that the product has been made in a way that treats the workers fairly

Fairtrade bananas can be found in many supermarkets. Bananas are now the favourite fruit, more popular than apples. They are the third best-selling product in supermarkets. (Petrol and lottery tickets are first and second.) Supermarket owners want to keep the price of bananas low. They want to buy their bananas from companies that are cheap. Some companies save money by not giving the workers enough money or proper safety equipment. When supermarkets sell Fairtrade bananas, people in the UK can choose to buy their bananas from companies that they know treat the workers fairly.

The Rugmark is another example of fair trading. It is a label put on rugs to show that they were not made by small children. In the Developing World, children sometimes as young as six or seven work for long hours in factories, making rugs to sell to people in rich countries. They do not get enough fresh air and exercise. Often it harms their health. They cannot go to school, which often stops them from getting a better job when they are older.

EDUCATION AND CHILD LABOUR

In very poor countries, fewer than half the adults can read and write. Most children never go to secondary school. Many of the people who cannot read are women. This is because families often cannot afford to send all their children to school, so they just send the boys. Boys will have to earn a living when they grow up, but girls could work in the home. Women work in the fields growing crops, and then they work in the home doing the cooking, cleaning and washing. Girls are often kept at home to help their mothers. They might have to do this work when girls in richer countries are still in infant classes.

Child labour is a big problem in the Developing World. In the year 2000, more than 250 million children between the ages of five and 14 were working. Some work in factories, some in fields, some on the streets. Their parents need the money. If they went to school they would not have any wages. So they never learn enough to get a better job. UNICEF is an organisation that tries to make sure children under 14 do not have to work. It tries to get money for the families, so that they can afford to send the children to school.

If people have no education, it is hard for them to change the way they live. There are not many good jobs for people who

CHRISTIAN RESPONSIBILITY TOWARDS DISADVANTAGED PEOPLE

Child labour is a great problem in Developing Countries. This child has little hope of an education

cannot read or write. It also makes other things more difficult, such as getting the right health care.

Many people who work for aid agencies say that the rich need educating, as well as the poor. The poor need to learn basic skills, to help them read instructions so that they can work machines and know how to take their medicines. They need to learn when they are being cheated out of money. But the rich need to learn, too. They need to learn how the things they do affect people in poor countries. People in the North do not often plan to buy things that come from companies which cheat the poor. But they do not always know what is going on. Aid agencies often spend part of their money on education for rich countries. They want to tell rich countries to change the way they live, so that things can get better for the poor.

FOR DISCUSSION

Do you think that if you knew more about the Developing World, it would change the way that you live?

CHRISTIAN PERSPECTIVES

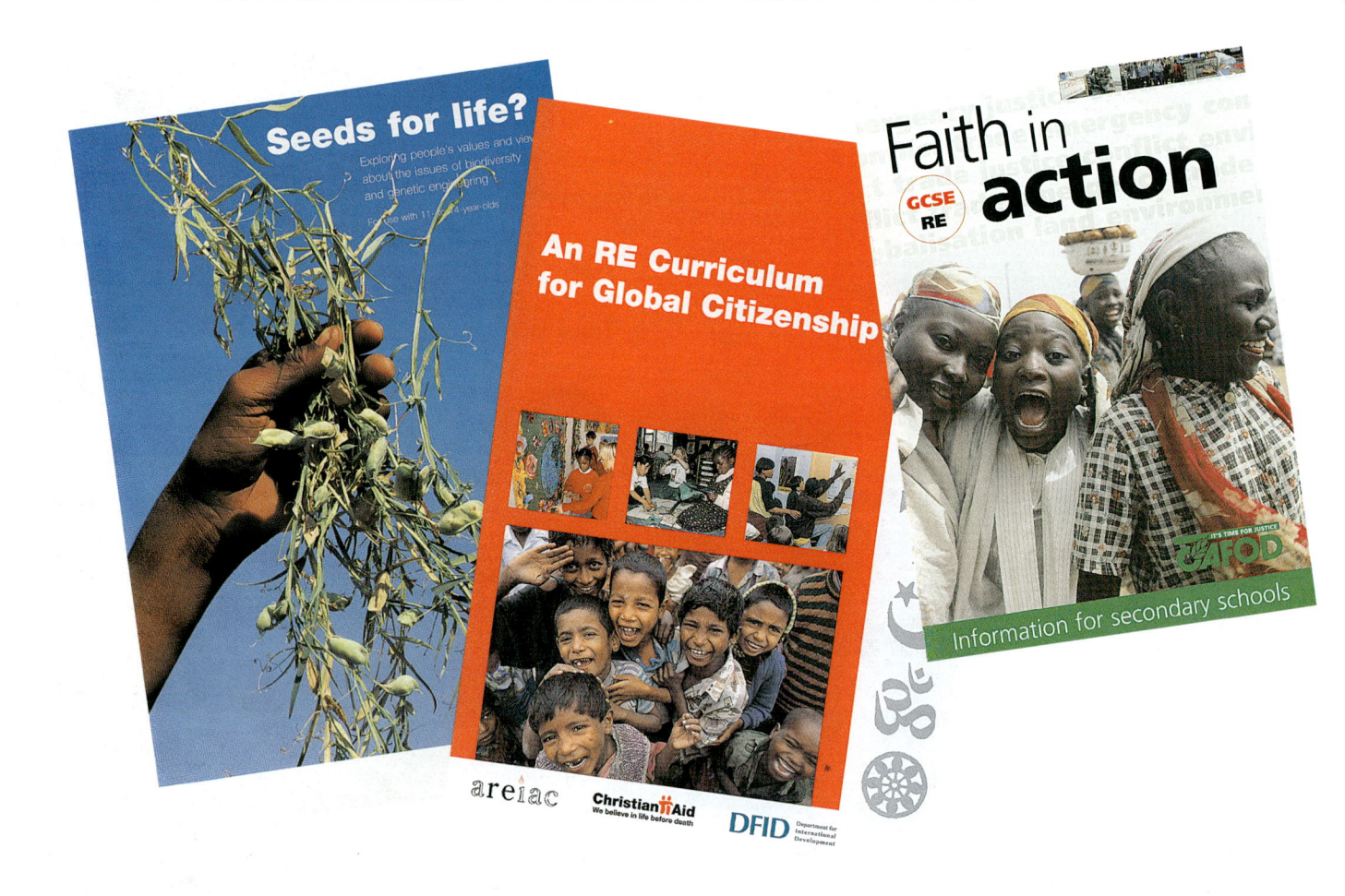

Many aid agencies spend some of their money on education for the rich. They think this is very important to help things change

POVERTY IN THE UK

There are poor people in the UK, as well as in developing countries. They are not as poor as people in other parts of the world, and not many people in the UK die of hunger. But there is still a big difference between the ways rich and poor people live in the UK. In the 1980s, the gap between rich and poor got bigger. The poor earned less, and the richest 20% of people got even richer.

About one in three children in the UK lives in poverty – a total of 4.5 million. Their families cannot give them the basic things they need. Over a million children live in homes where both parents do not have jobs.

When there is a big gap between rich and poor, it means things are unequal in lots of ways. Children from families without much money often do not do as well in school. This is sometimes because they do not have a quiet place at home where they can study, and they might have to do jobs such as

CHRISTIAN RESPONSIBILITY TOWARDS DISADVANTAGED PEOPLE

working on a market stall, to help out with money at home. They are more likely to live in houses or flats that are damp or cold and make them ill. They are more likely to get involved in crime or drugs, because they have to live in areas where these things go on all around them. Of course, not all people from low income families do badly at school or commit crimes. But it is much more difficult for them to do well, compared to children from rich families.

The Salvation Army is an example of a Christian organisation that works to help people in the UK. It has branches all over the world. It is famous for its work with the poor and the homeless in the UK. The government does the most to help poor people, and the second biggest helper is The Salvation Army. It provides shelters and hostels for homeless people, so that they have somewhere safe and clean where they can sleep at night. It runs a 'Missing Persons' network, to help people get in touch with their families if they have left home. It provides care for elderly people, with homes for them, and clubs where they can meet for a cup of tea and a chat so that they are not lonely. There are children's homes, and there is help for people who look after children with special needs.

People in The Salvation Army believe that Christianity means nothing unless it is put into action. They believe that one of the best ways of telling people about Christian love is to go out and do it.

The Salvation Army works among people in need

ICT FOR RESEARCH

Visit the Salvation Army website:

www.salvationarmy.org.uk

Find out more about the ways in which The Salvation Army works with people in the UK. Read about the beliefs of members of The Salvation Army, and find out how the organisation began in Victorian times.

105

CHRISTIAN PERSPECTIVES

BIBLICAL TEACHING ABOUT CARING FOR THE POOR

In the Old Testament in the Bible, there are many laws given by God which tell people that they must take care of the poor and treat them fairly:

> *Do not take advantage of a widow or an orphan… If you lend money to one of my people among you who is needy, do not be like a money-lender; charge him no interest.* (Exodus 22: 21–22, 25)
>
> *When you reap the harvest of your land, do not reap to the very edges of your field or gather the gleanings of your harvest. **Leave them for the poor** and the alien. I am the LORD your God.* (Leviticus 23: 22)
>
> *If one of your countrymen becomes poor and is unable to support himself among you, help him as you would an alien or a temporary resident, so that he can continue to live among you … You must not lend him money at interest or sell him food at a profit.* (Leviticus 25: 35, 37)

These are just a few examples. Loving God means keeping the commandments. People were told over and over again that they should show love for God by caring for each other. They should have special care for people in need.

> *Whoever loves God must also love his brother.* (1 John 4: 21)

Amos was a prophet. The job of a prophet is to pass messages from God to the people. Amos was only an ordinary sheep-farmer, but he was a brilliant prophet. The message Amos gave everyone was quite clear. God was going to punish the people. God was not impressed by their worship, because they had been cheating the poor.

> *I hate, I despise your religious feasts; I cannot stand your assemblies … Away with the noise of your songs! I will not listen to the music of your harps. But **let justice roll on** like a river, righteousness like a never-failing stream!* (Amos 5: 21, 23–24)

Amos said that the people were so greedy that they did not think about God on the Sabbath. Instead, they wanted the Sabbath to be over quickly, so that they could get back to making money. They had been cheating people by fixing the scales in shops, so that people got less than they had paid for. They treated the poor as if they were worth less than a cheap pair of shoes.

> *Hear this, **you who trample the needy** and do away with the poor of the land, saying, 'When will the New Moon be over that we may sell grain, and the Sabbath be ended that we may market wheat?' – skimping the measure, boosting the price and cheating with dishonest scales, buying the poor with silver and the needy for a pair of sandals, selling even the sweepings with the wheat.* (Amos 8: 4–6)

Other prophets also said that God was angry with people who did nothing for the poor. Isaiah also spoke about showing love to people in need:

> *… and if you spend yourselves on behalf of the hungry and satisfy the needs of the oppressed, then your light will rise in the darkness, and your night will become like the noonday.* (Isaiah 58: 10)

In the New Testament, care for the poor is seen as very important, especially in Luke's Gospel. When Jesus began teaching, he told everyone what he believed he was meant to do:

CHRISTIAN RESPONSIBILITY TOWARDS DISADVANTAGED PEOPLE

> 'The spirit of the LORD is upon me, because he has anointed me **to preach good news to the poor.** He has sent me to proclaim freedom for the prisoners and recovery of sight for the blind, to release the oppressed, to proclaim the year of the LORD's favour.' (Luke 4: 18–19)

At the time of Jesus, many people thought that rich people had been rewarded by God, and should be respected. But Jesus taught something different:

> Looking at his disciples, he said: '**Blessed are you who are poor**, for yours is the kingdom of God. Blessed are you who hunger now, for you will be satisfied. Blessed are you who weep now, for you will laugh. (Luke 6: 20–21)

The poor were shown to be special to God.

Jesus taught that Christian love (agape) is not just a feeling. It has to be put into action. He said it is wrong to have expensive things when there are poor people around who need help. It goes against the teaching of the Two Greatest Commandments:

> Love the LORD your God with all your heart and with all your soul and with all your mind and with all your strength ... **Love your neighbour as yourself.** (Mark 12: 30–31)

There are two parables in particular which teach that it is very wrong to do nothing for the poor. In Luke's Gospel, the parable of Dives and Lazarus shows how a rich man is punished because he ignores the poor man who is begging at his gate:

> There was a rich man who was dressed in purple and fine linen and lived in luxury every day. At his gate was laid a beggar named Lazarus, covered with sores and longing to eat what fell from the rich man's table. Even the dogs came and licked his sores.
>
> The time came when the beggar died and the angels carried him to Abraham's side. The rich man also died and was buried.
>
> In hell, where he was in torment, he looked up and saw Abraham far away, with Lazarus by his side.
>
> So he called to him, 'Father Abraham, have pity on me and send Lazarus to dip the tip of his finger in water and cool my tongue, because I am in agony in this fire.'
>
> But Abraham replied, 'Son, remember that in your lifetime you received your good things, while Lazarus received bad things, but now he is comforted here and you are in agony.
>
> And besides all this, between us and you a great chasm has been fixed, so that those who want to go from here to you cannot, nor can anyone cross over from there to us.'
>
> He answered, 'Then I beg you, father, send Lazarus to my father's house,
> for I have five brothers. Let him warn them, so that they will not also come to this place of torment.'
>
> Abraham replied, 'They have Moses and the Prophets; let them listen to them.'
>
> 'No, father Abraham,' he said, 'but if someone from the dead goes to them, they will repent.'
>
> He said to him, 'If they do not listen to Moses and the Prophets, they will not be convinced even if someone rises from the dead.' (Luke 16: 19–31)

The rich man says that he wants to warn his brothers about the need to care for the poor. But he is reminded that the prophets have been saying this for years.

In Matthew's Gospel, the parable of the Sheep and the Goats says that caring for the poor is the same as caring for Jesus. Doing nothing for the poor is the same as doing nothing for Jesus:

CHRISTIAN PERSPECTIVES

IN YOUR NOTES

Look up the story in Mark 10: 17–22.
(a) What did the rich young man ask Jesus?
(b) What answer did Jesus give him?

FOR DISCUSSION

Do you think that Christians today should give all their money to the poor?

Christians believe that caring for the poor is a very important part of their faith

> When the Son of Man comes in his glory, and all the angels with him, he will sit on his throne in heavenly glory. All the nations will be gathered before him, and he will separate the people one from another as a shepherd separates the sheep from the goats.
>
> He will put the sheep on his right and the goats on his left.
>
> Then the King will say to those on his right, 'Come, you who are blessed by my Father; take your inheritance, the kingdom prepared for you since the creation of the world.
>
> For I was hungry and you gave me something to eat, I was thirsty and you gave me something to drink, I was a stranger and you invited me in,
>
> I needed clothes and you clothed me, I was sick and you looked after me, I was in prison and you came to visit me.'
>
> Then the righteous will answer him, 'Lord, when did we see you hungry and feed you, or thirsty and give you something to drink?
>
> When did we see you a stranger and invite you in, or needing clothes and clothe you?
>
> When did we see you sick or in prison and go to visit you?'
>
> The King will reply, 'I tell you the truth, **whatever you did for one of the least of these brothers of mine, you did for me.'**
>
> Then he will say to those on his left, 'Depart from me, you who are cursed, into the eternal fire prepared for the devil and his angels.
>
> For I was hungry and you gave me nothing to eat, I was thirsty and you gave me nothing to drink,
>
> I was a stranger and you did not invite me in, I needed clothes and you did not clothe me, I was sick and in prison and you did not look after me.'
>
> They also will answer, 'Lord, when did we see you hungry or thirsty or a stranger or needing clothes or sick or in prison, and did not help you?'
>
> He will reply, 'I tell you the truth, **whatever you did not do for one of the least of these, you did not do for me.'**
>
> Then they will go away to eternal punishment, but the righteous to eternal life.
>
> (Matthew 25: 31–46)

Christians believe that it is their duty to care for people in need. It shows the belief that everyone is made 'in the image of God' (Genesis 1: 27), so everyone matters to God.

IN YOUR NOTES

Write two paragraphs explaining what the Bible teaches about caring for the poor. Use some short quotations in your writing, as examples, but do not copy out long passages. Try to put the ideas in your own words.

CHRISTIAN RESPONSIBILITY TOWARDS DISADVANTAGED PEOPLE

CHRISTIAN BELIEFS IN ACTION

There are many different ways in which Christians could show love for the poor. For example:

- They might spend their lives working with the poor in a developing country, maybe as an aid worker, or a doctor or nurse.
- They might give part of their lives to work for the poor, perhaps for a year when they are students. They could work with an organisation such as Voluntary Service Overseas, which sends people with skills to the places they are most needed, for two or three years.
- They could help in this country, to support the work of others in developing countries. For example, they could work for a charity in a shop or collecting money. They could take part in events to raise money, such as sponsored walks, marathon running or coffee mornings.
- A Christian could try to live a simple life and not have the most fashionable clothes, and not spend a lot on going out. The money saved could be given to charity.
- Christians might try not to waste things. They could save money on fuel and food. They could give their old books and clothes to charity shops, rather than throwing them away.
- Christians could try to buy goods that have a Fairtrade mark. They could avoid buying from companies that do not treat the poor well. They could try to do business with companies that have a good record in caring for the poor.
- Many Christians support the poor and the people who work with them through prayer.
- Christians could give money to charity on a regular basis. Some give spare cash when they are asked. Others keep charity collection boxes in their homes and put their spare change in them. Some Christians give part of their income to the poor and the church. Some arrange with their bank to pay an agreed amount every month – charities like this form of giving, because they can get tax benefits, and they can plan for the future because they know how much money is coming each month. Many Christians leave money to charities when they die.

FOR DISCUSSION

How much money do you think people in the Developed World should give to poorer countries?

Putting Christian beliefs into action

CHRISTIAN PERSPECTIVES

AID AGENCIES

Many people help charities, whether they are Christian or not. There are many aid agencies which are not Christian and do not come from any religious background. People just want to do something to help the poor. Organisations such as Oxfam, Save the Children Fund, Comic Relief and others are not Christian, but they do a lot to help the poor.

In Christianity, helping the poor is not just something people might choose to do, if they are feeling kind. It is a duty, something they must do.

> What good is it, my brothers, if a man claims to have faith but has no deeds? Can such faith save him? Suppose a brother or a sister is without clothes and daily food. If one of you says to him, 'Go, I wish you well; keep warm and well fed,' but does nothing about his physical needs, what good is it? In the same way, **faith by itself, if it is not accompanied by action, is dead.** (James 2: 14–16)

Some Christians have started aid agencies because of this belief. They try to put Christian teaching into action.

CHRISTIAN RESPONSIBILITY TOWARDS DISADVANTAGED PEOPLE

TRAIDCRAFT

Traidcraft is a Christian organisation. It was started in 1979, with the aim of making trade conditions better for the poor, and caring for the environment. It says that it wants to:

'put people before profit.'

Traidcraft sells handicrafts, fashion goods, stationery, tea, coffee, cocoa and foods produced by developing countries. It works with the poor as partners, to help them become independent. The company tells the workers about goods which are likely to sell, and it pays in advance, so that the poor can buy the materials they need without going hungry.

ICT FOR RESEARCH

Visit the Traidcraft web-site to look at the products for sale and to find out more about the people who produce them: www.traidcraft.co.uk

IN YOUR NOTES

Explain some of the main features of Fairtrade companies like Traidcraft. Show how the company tries to put its principles into action.

Traidcraft aims to help people become independent by producing goods which can be sold fairly

CHRISTIAN PERSPECTIVES

CHRISTIAN AID

Christian Aid
We believe in life before death

HISTORY

Christian Aid is an aid agency that represents over 40 different Churches in the UK and Ireland. It was formed after the Second World War, to help people who had lost their homes and families. There were many refugees who had nothing. The Churches joined together and raised over a million pounds, which was a huge amount just after the war when people had little to give. Work began to help the refugees.

During the 1950s and 1960s, Europe was at peace. The Churches began to work in other countries where people were very poor, especially in Africa. The name became Christian Aid.

- In the 1970s, Christian Aid helped people who had survived an earthquake in Peru. It helped people in India who had no water, and people in Sudan and East Pakistan who had no food.
- In the 1980s, Christian Aid helped the victims of war in Lebanon. It sent doctors and nurses to help people who were hurt. It helped people in Ethiopia, and gave them food, water, schools and health care.
- In the 1990s, Christian Aid worked for fair trade, and for an end to world debt. It worked to make people more aware of child labour and the child sex industry. Christian Aid helped people in wars in Rwanda, Yugoslavia and Sierra Leone.

Today, Christian Aid works in more than 70 countries, on more than 700 local projects.

THE ROLE OF CHRISTIAN AID

Christian Aid is known for helping when there is a disaster, such as a flood, or an earthquake, or a famine. But helping in emergencies is not the main part of Christian Aid's work. It tries

Aid workers try to help refugees who have nowhere to go because of war

CHRISTIAN RESPONSIBILITY TOWARDS DISADVANTAGED PEOPLE

ICT FOR RESEARCH
Visit the Christian Aid web-site
www.christian-aid.org.uk/
Find out more about the work of Christian Aid. Choose one or two of the projects that Christian Aid is working on today, and read about them. Write some notes about the projects, so that you can use them as examples in your answers.

Christian Aid is keen to support women's projects

to help things change over a long time, rather than just waiting for a crisis to happen. It tries to give people skills and education, so that they can help themselves and do not always need other people's charity.

As well as providing food for emergencies, Christian Aid teaches people about farming. It helps them to grow better crops so that they can manage on their own. It helps to get fair wages for workers. It gives medicines when there is disease, and it also teaches people how to be more healthy. It trains people to be nurses, and shows them how to deliver babies safely. It shows people how to stop diseases from spreading. It gives education for children and adults. Christian Aid tries hard to support women, because they are often left to bring up families on their own if their husbands are killed in wars. The women are taught new skills so that they can make things to sell.

CHRISTIAN AID FUND-RAISING
Christian Aid puts in a lot of effort for Christian Aid Week, in May each year. In this week there are adverts on television, posters, church collections, street collections, and envelopes delivered to people's homes. People who do not give to Christian Aid the rest of the year often give something in Christian Aid Week.

Christian Aid also raises money at other times of the year. People give money, and leave money in their wills when they die. They sell goods such as Christmas cards, and money is raised through events such as sponsored walks.

CHRISTIAN PERSPECTIVES

CARITAS

Caritas is a Roman Catholic aid organisation, for more than 150 countries around the world. It does not just give help to Catholics. It helps anyone who is in need. Caritas works for people who have no power, for the homeless, the hungry, and anyone else who needs help. Caritas Internationalis finds out where help is needed, and gets in touch with churches in different parts of the world to make sure that the right help is given as quickly as possible.

Caritas says it is not enough to give food, clothing and medicines. People have to be helped to live independently. They should not be made to feel that they always have to beg for help.

The Catholic Church teaches that:

> *If faith is not expressed in works, it is dead* (cf. James 2: 14–16) *and cannot bear fruit unto eternal life.*
>
> (Catechism of the Catholic Church)

ICT FOR RESEARCH

Visit the web-site of Caritas Internationalis www.caritas.org Find out about its work in different parts of the world. You might want to see how it works in places such as Kosovo, Romania and Zambia.

CAFOD

The branch of Caritas in England and Wales is called CAFOD (Catholic Agency for Overseas Development). It helps more than a thousand projects around the world. It aims to get rid of poverty and provide fair shares for everyone.

CAFOD works with people in developing countries as partners. It also works in England and Wales in parishes, schools and community groups, to help people understand more about poverty.

CAFOD is based on the Christian belief that everyone is made in the image of God. It says Christians should see Christ in each person. It says that it wants to see a world where:

- Everyone has a fair share of the good things in the world.
- The rights of each person are respected. People do not discriminate against each other, they live together as a family, and no one is left out.
- People listen to the poor, and do not put greed first.
- Everyone is able to get food, shelter, clean water, a job, good health and education.

CHRISTIAN RESPONSIBILITY TOWARDS DISADVANTAGED PEOPLE

HISTORY

CAFOD was started to put Christian beliefs into action. It began in a small way. People in a Caribbean island asked for help with a mother and baby health project. Some Catholic women in the UK decided to help them by having a Family Fast Day. This is when people go without food for a day, and give the money they would have spent on meals to the poor. Fasting is still one of CAFOD's main ways of raising money. Sometimes, people are sponsored to fast. In this way, they do not just give money, but also feel what it is like to be hungry, and it helps them care more about hungry people.

In 1962, CAFOD was formed, by the Catholic Bishops of England and Wales. They wanted to bring together all the fund-raising work that was already going on. They wanted to make it easier for people to know about problems in the world, and to make the fund-raising more organised.

After just ten years, CAFOD was helping 245 projects in 40 countries. Like Christian Aid, CAFOD tries to help people become independent. It wants to start them off so that they can manage on their own and not need charity any more.

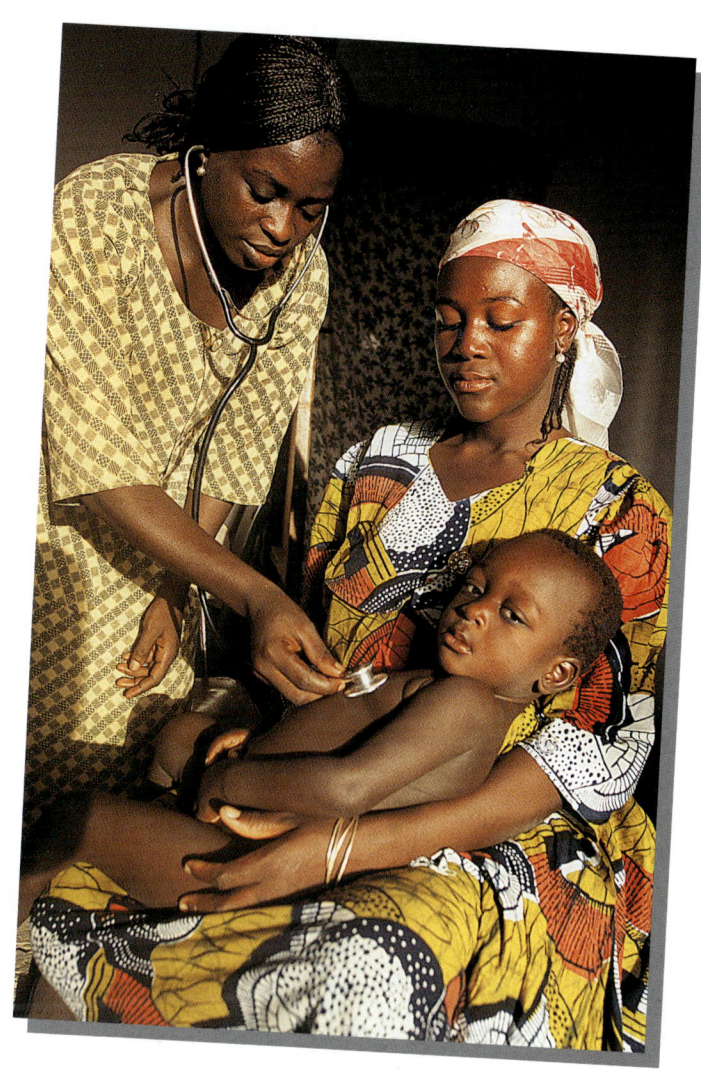

Healthcare is a major concern for CAFOD

ICT FOR RESEARCH

Visit the CAFOD web-site:
www.cafod.org.uk/
Find out more about the work of CAFOD. Look at its work in fair trade, and in trying to cancel debt. Look at the work it does in trying to stop people using landmines, and its work with refugees. Find out more about the reasons why Christians might choose to support CAFOD.

CHRISTIAN PERSPECTIVES

TEARFUND

Tearfund began when there was a civil war in Nigeria, in 1968. Hundreds of people were left dead, and many more were starving. People began sending money to a group of Christians called the Evangelical Alliance, so that they could help the Nigerians. They set up a fund, called The Evangelical Relief Fund – now known as Tearfund. When it started, it raised £34,000, and today it raises over £20 million each year.

Tearfund is a Christian relief and development charity. 'Relief' means that it gives help in emergencies, so that people have the things they need to survive, such as food, medicines and blankets. 'Development' means it also works in ways that will last a long time, such as giving education. Like CAFOD and Christian Aid, it treats people in developing countries as partners. It tries to work with them, not just for them. It tries to give them the skills they need so that they can help themselves.

Tearfund believes that the poor matter just as much as the rich. It believes that everyone is made in the image of God. It does not matter what colour, religion or sex they are. It believes that the poor should be shown respect.

Tearfund runs many different projects in developing countries. It sends volunteers to refugee camps in places where there have been wars, and gives the refugees food, shelter and medical supplies. In India and Africa, it helps people who have HIV and AIDS. In Haiti, it gives education to children from poor families. If they did not have this help, they could not go to school.

Tearfund also has a UK Action Fund, to help churches in the UK work with poor people.

ICT FOR RESEARCH

Visit the Tearfund web-site:
www.tearfund.org
Find out more about the work of Tearfund. Look at some of the projects that are going on today, to use as examples in your writing. Find out how Tearfund tries to put Christian beliefs into action.

Christians believe that all human beings are made 'in the image of God', and deserve fair shares

CHRISTIAN RESPONSIBILITY TOWARDS DISADVANTAGED PEOPLE

PRACTICE EXAMINATION QUESTIONS

1 (a) **Describe the work of a Christian organisation which helps the poor in developing countries. (8 marks)**

   Remember to choose an organisation that is Christian – some are not. You might want to choose Christian Aid, CAFOD or Tearfund. This question asks you to describe the work, so you need to say what the organisation does, and not write too much about other aspects such as its history.

   (b) **Explain how Christians might show concern for the poor in their daily lives. (7 marks)**

   This question is about how Christians might put their faith into action, and show care for the poor. You need to think about different ways they could do this. Try to mention several different ideas. Prayer is often a good idea to use in part (b) answers. You might also want to look at some of the ideas on page 109.

   (c) **'It is not our responsibility if people in other countries are starving.' Do you agree? Give reasons to support your answer, and show that you have thought about different points of view. You must refer to Christianity in your answer. (5 marks)**

   Remember that for full marks, you need to think and write about what a Christian would say. Then write about what someone might say if they disagreed with a Christian. You need to give your own view, with reasons.

2 (a) **Describe Christian teaching about care for the poor. (8 marks)**

   There are a lot of different ideas you could use here. You could use teaching from the Bible, and from different Churches, and from Christian organisations such as Christian Aid, CAFOD and Tearfund. When you are writing about teaching from the Bible, you do not have to be able to remember all the right words exactly. You can refer to teaching such as 'the Parable of the Sheep and the Goats' without telling the whole story.

   (b) **Explain how a Christian might support the work of an organisation which deals with problems of world hunger. (7 marks)**

   Notice that this time, you are asked how a Christian might support an aid organisation. So you do not need to write a lot about the organisation itself. What you need to write about is how a Christian might support it in different ways, such as by working in a charity shop, collecting money, praying or fasting.

   (c) **'Christians should give away all their money to the poor.' Do you agree? Give reasons to support your answer, and show that you have thought about different points of view. (5 marks)**

   Remember to support each point of view with reasons. You might write about how a Christian would feel about this statement. Perhaps you could include some teaching from the Bible here. You might then write about why someone else might disagree with this view. Remember to give your own view as well, and say why this is what you think.

RELIGION, THE MEDIA AND ENTERTAINMENT

Knowledge of various issues and an understanding of them in the relationship between Religion, the Media and Entertainment. Knowledge of the religious basis for the issues raised.

Today, people who live in rich countries have all sorts of media. There are televisions, radios, newspapers, the Internet, cinemas, videos and DVDs, CD-ROMs, posters and advertisements. Every day, we see the media all around us. It is the main way we learn of news in the world, and a favourite form of entertainment.

The media is a way for people to share their beliefs and opinions. They can try to change other people's minds, using the media.

Christians think that the media has some **good points:**

- Television and radio can be a good way for Christians to share their faith with a large number of others. Christians can tell other people about their beliefs using the media.

The media plays an important part in modern life

RELIGION, THE MEDIA AND ENTERTAINMENT

- Religious programmes give people a chance to join in with Christian worship, even if they cannot get to church. If they are old, or ill, or have small children, they can watch a church service or listen to it, from their homes.
- The media can be used to teach people. Many people learn about problems in the world through the media. They find out about the environment, and what they can do to help. They find out when there are famines, or floods, or earthquakes. Some people are very affected by the things they see and hear, and they want to do something about it. They might give money to the poor, or go to countries such as Romania to take help, because of the things they have seen in the media. Christians believe it is important to know what is going on in the world, so that they can pray about it and try to help when people are in need.
- The media often discusses religious and moral questions. Christians can use these discussions to explain a Christian point of view. Some Christians also think that when television dramas have stories about issues such as abortion or homelessness, it is a good chance to talk about these topics at home with the rest of the family.
- Charities and other groups, such as Christian Aid, Amnesty International or Tearfund, can use the media to tell people about the work they do. They use web-sites, television and newspaper advertisements to make people more aware of their work. Some groups, such as the Samaritans, even do some of their work using the Internet. People can e-mail their problems and receive support in this way.

Some Christians believe that the media also has **bad points**:

- Watching television and using the Internet can make people spend too much time on their own. People spend a lot of time watching television, and they could use this time to talk to each other. In the evenings, many families sit in front of the television without saying a word to each other, even when they are eating.
- The media sometimes gives a view of the world that does not fit in with Christian teachings. In many television drama series, for example, the main characters are married and divorced several times. They have affairs and they commit crimes. The stories are interesting and entertaining, but they give the idea that everyone behaves like this. People might copy this.
- Some Christians think that the media makes people more violent. They do not like it when violence is used to entertain people.
- Many Christians think pornography is wrong. They think it can often give the idea that women are here to be used by men, and they think it can give a wrong idea about what sex is for. People in control of the media often make a lot of money from pornography, especially on the Internet.
- Christians can use the media to share their beliefs and opinions, but so can people who disagree with Christianity. Some programmes make fun of Christianity and of church leaders.
- Adverts can make people greedy. They can make people want more than they really need. They can make people feel bad if they are not as rich as other people. Many Christians think that advertising gives people the wrong idea about what is important in life.
- The people who own the media want to sell their products. Sometimes, sales can become more important than other things, such as people's privacy or feelings. The media might publish something to make some money, even if it hurts people by saying too much about their private lives.

CHRISTIAN PERSPECTIVES

Some people believe that television prevents families from talking to each other

FOR DISCUSSION

Do you think it is right for Christian parents to try to control what their children watch on television?

Some Christians believe that the media has such a bad effect on family life and on Christian values that they do not own televisions and do not buy newspapers. But most Christians do not feel this way. They watch television, buy newspapers and use the Internet, but they are careful about what they choose. Christian parents are likely to try and control the things their children watch and read, to make sure they are right for the children's age, and that they say the right things.

Christians have always used the media to explain their beliefs. The Gospel stories were written down and passed around the early Christians. Christians used letters to tell others about what it meant to be a Christian. Today, there are very many more methods that Christians can use to share their beliefs with other people.

FOR DISCUSSION

If Christianity was beginning today, rather than 2000 years ago, what methods do you think the first believers would use to publicise their message?

RELIGION, THE MEDIA AND ENTERTAINMENT

EXPRESSING CHRISTIAN BELIEFS IN ART

Art is one of the oldest forms of media. Some religions teach that it is very wrong to use art to try and show God or important religious people. But many Christians think that it helps to use art. They think that using things like pictures, stained glass, sculpture and needlework help to bring religious ideas to life.

Some Christians think it is better to have simple, plain places to worship. Christians such as Quakers and Baptists think that plain churches are better, because they do not distract people.

Some Christian churches use a lot of art, to help people think about God in different ways

CHRISTIAN PERSPECTIVES

Some of the greatest art in the world has come from Christian painters. When people look at the ways in which different artists imagine Jesus, or a story from the Bible, it can help them understand in a new way.

RELIGIOUS BROADCASTS

Christians often use television and radio as a way of sharing their beliefs. Special religious programmes are often called the 'God slot'. They are at a special time of day, or a special time in the week. Many Christians enjoy these. But some people think that religious programmes should not have a special time of their own. They think it might seem as though religion is different from ordinary life. So they prefer to have religious ideas mixed in with other programmes, and not kept apart.

Christians have always used art as a way of expressing their beliefs. Crucifixion *by Rubens*

TELEVISION EVANGELISM

'Television evangelism' is popular with some Christians. These are programmes where a preacher explains his or her beliefs about Christianity. There is often singing and prayers. Sometimes, the viewers are asked to send money to support the work of the programme.

Some Christians think that television evangelism is a good way of telling people about Christianity. Other people do not like it, because the preacher might explain Christianity in a way that not all Christians like. Some people think that these programmes ask for money too often, and they do not always use it in ways that all Christians would support.

ACTS OF WORSHIP

During the week, there are programmes on the radio and television which are called 'acts of worship'. They are live broadcasts of religious services. People who watch or listen can hear the sermon, and join in with the hymns and prayers. Many

ICT FOR RESEARCH

Visit the web-site of the BBC:
www.bbc.co.uk/
Go to the 'what's on' page, and select 'Religion and Beliefs'. How many religious programmes are on BBC television and radio this week? Apart from religious worship, what other sorts of religious programmes are there?

RELIGION, THE MEDIA AND ENTERTAINMENT

Christians enjoy *Songs of Praise* on a Sunday, or listening to the daily service on Radio 4. They like to hear carols from King's College, Cambridge on Christmas Eve. These programmes might help Christians to think more about their faith. They might make Christians think about being part of a whole community of Christians in different parts of the world.

But some people might think that it is not a good idea to have acts of worship on the radio or on television. They think it could make people less interested in going to church. They might not bother, if they have seen a church service on the television or heard it on the radio, so they might miss the chance to worship with other Christians.

LOOK UP

Look in the television section of the newspaper, or in the *Radio Times* or *TV Times*, and find out more about the religious programmes that are on this week. Are other religions represented, as well as Christianity?

Televised acts of worship can be enjoyed by people who are unable to get to church

DISCUSSION PROGRAMMES

Some discussion programmes include Christian views. A moral or social issue is raised for people to discuss. This might be something like euthanasia, or attitudes to people in other countries. Often, one or more of the people on the panel is a Christian. This person tries to put forward a Christian point of view. Most Christians support this kind of programme, because they see it as a good opportunity for people to hear that Christianity has something to say about modern issues.

ADVERTISING

Advertising is an important part of society in developed countries. There are adverts on television, at cinemas, in newspapers and magazines, on buses, at sports events, on the Internet and in many other places. We see adverts every day.

Sometimes, advertising can be a good thing. It shows us products that could make our lives easier. It sometimes shows us how we could save money. Many charities spend some of their money on advertising, so that people know what work they do and how to give money. Christian churches often advertise. They might put posters up, to tell people what is going on in the church. Some churches advertise with newsletters, which they deliver to people's houses.

Often, advertising can be a bad thing. It can make people think they should spend more than they can afford. Adverts make people think they need to buy the product so that they will be attractive and successful and have lots of friends. They try to make people feel that they are missing something. They suggest that there is something wrong with having grey hair, or a second-hand car, or clothes that you wore last year. They try to make us think that other people are having more fun than we are. Adverts try to make us spend more and more on ourselves, even though three quarters of the world have far less than we do.

People who have low incomes often have problems with adverts. Their children start wanting things that the parents cannot afford. Just before Christmas, children are shown adverts for expensive toys. They are made to think that everyone else will be getting these toys. This can be hard for the parents.

Adverts can also cause problems with prejudice. Advertisers who want to show a happy family nearly always choose a white family. This gives the idea that 'normal' families are white. Adverts also often make people think that women are only interested in housework, and men do outdoor jobs.

FILMS ABOUT CHRISTIANITY

Some Christians believe it is wrong to make films about the life of Jesus. They say he was such a special and important person that it would be wrong to get an actor to pretend to be Jesus, and it would be wrong to try and draw him for an animation or make a puppet of him. Sometimes, people leave a bit out of the story, or add a bit in, to make the film fit together better, and Christians might say it is wrong to do this with the Bible. Some films do not stick to the story very closely. Some use the Bible as a basis for a comedy. Christians might be offended by this.

Other people think that films of the story of Jesus can be a good way of bringing it to life. People can imagine what it must have been

RELIGION, THE MEDIA AND ENTERTAINMENT

like to see Jesus perform a miracle or hear him teach. Often, when Christians read the Bible, they just read a small part at a time, but a film can give the whole story and make more of an impact.

People might not like reading books very much, but they might enjoy seeing films and find them easier to understand. Films can be a good way of getting people to think about what Christianity has to say.

has a lot of influence on the ways people think. It helps to shape our opinions. Christians and non-Christians think that not everything in the media is good.

CONCLUSION

Christians are not against the media. The media is just a collection of ways of communicating. But sometimes, Christians are worried about what the media says. The media

'The Miracle Maker' is a film of the life of Jesus, presented in animation

INDEX

abortion:
   Biblical teaching 38
   Church teaching 38–9
   Christian responses 39–40
   the law 37, 40
   organisations 40–1
agape 9–10
Amnesty International 82–4
apartheid 57–9
Augustine, St 11
Bible, use of by Christians 2, 4
Bonhoeffer, Dietrich 8
Brandt report 97
CAFOD 114–15
CARITAS 114
Christian Aid 112–13
Church, role of 5–6
CMAC 26
conscience 7
contraception 32–3
creation 86–7
Dives and Lazarus, parable of 107
divorce 22–4
environment:
   problems 90–2
   Christian responses 93–4

euthanasia:
   Church teaching 48
   the law 46
Fair Trade 100–2
family life:
   roles of children and parents 20
   roles of men and women 18–19
   importance of 12–13
fertility treatment 34–5
Fletcher, Joseph 11
Good Samaritan, parable of 62
Greatest Commandments 9
Holy Spirit 8
hospice movement 49–50
Huddleston, Trevor 58–9
human rights 79–80
Liberation theology 80–1
Luther King Jnr, Martin 60–1
Macmillan nurses 50
marriage:
   Biblical teaching about 15
   Christian service 16
   importance of 14, 24
media 118–25
Mothers' Union 24–5
non-violence 78–9

North-South divide 96
poverty:
   Biblical teaching 106–8
   causes 98
   Christian responses 109–16
prayer, importance of 7
prejudice, Christian teaching 62–4
racism 52–6
Relate 25
Romero, Oscar 81–2
Salvation Army 105
Samaritans 44–5
sanctity of life 30
Sermon on the Mount 3
sexism 65–9
Sheep and Goats, parable of 107–8
stewardship 87–9
suicide 32, 42–3
Tearfund 116
Ten Commandments 2–3
Torres, Camilo 81
Traidcraft 111
war:
   Biblical teaching 73–4
   Church teaching 75–8
   Just War 75
   pacifism 78